EVERYDAY ENGLISH

Everyday English

Getting to Grips with the
Basics of the Language

Michelle Finlay

MICHAEL O'MARA BOOKS LIMITED

First published in Great Britain in 2011 by
Michael O'Mara Books Limited
9 Lion Yard
Tremadoc Road
London SW4 7NQ

A CIP catalogue record for this book is available from
the British Library.

Papers used by Michael O'Mara Books Limited are natural, recy-
clable products made from wood grown in sustainable forests. The
manufacturing processes conform to the environmental regulations
of the country of origin.

ISBN: 978-1-84317-566-7 in hardback print format
ISBN: 978-1-84317 978-1-84317-680-0 in EPub format
ISBN: 978-1-84317-681-7 in Mobipocket format

1 2 3 4 5 6 7 8 9 10

Cover design by Patrick Knowles
Designed and typeset by Ed Pickford
Illustrations by Andrew Pinder

Printed and bound in Great Britain by Clays Ltd, St Ives plc

www.mombooks.com

For Michael: words fail me

Contents

Introduction

Good English is everywhere. It is not the preserve of the BBC or of our greatest writers. It may be heard in everyday conversation, and can be found in magazine or newspaper articles, in press releases, political speeches, instruction manuals or advertisements, and elsewhere.

Sadly, the opposite is also true. English is often brought to its knees by tabloid headlines, company reports, websites, DVD subtitles – and also by press releases, instruction manuals and advertisements ...

None of us is immune to the odd mistake; very few of us can hold up our hands and say we never make an error or find ourselves hesitating over a word or a point of grammar. The problem is that if standards around us fall, we tend to fall with them. There is something about seeing a word or phrase in print that gives it credibility, whether it deserves it or not, and if we see the same mistake over and over again, we begin to see it as acceptable.

Everyday English

You might ask if it matters that we make mistakes in grammar, that we punctuate badly and confuse our tenses. I believe it matters a great deal. Civilization is based on communication; faulty communication leads to misunderstanding and can impede progress. As the world has developed, so has language, and quite rightly. Where would we be without new words for scientific discoveries, new technology and new concepts? Unfortunately, this has introduced a whole raft of new errors and abuses into the English language. Of course, we must move forward, but we should try to do so without losing any of the clarity and scope for expression that a good grasp of the language provides.

English is one of the richest, most colourful and most subtle languages in the world. To speak or write good English – plain, lucid, jargon-free English – to have mastery of the language, is to have style.

English speakers are blessed with the good fortune to share their language with some of the finest writers and orators of all time. As well as including hundreds of everyday examples of correct English, I have turned to great writers, from Jane Austen to Oscar Wilde, for inspiration.

Imitating such masters, however, this is more easily said than done. This is where this book comes in. *Everyday English* is designed to help native and non-native English speakers alike gain command of the language. Beginning with the letters of the alphabet, the book works its way, little by little, from the building blocks of written and spoken English – spelling, word order, punctuation, parts of speech – to tone of voice, pitfalls to avoid, and tips to ensure clarity, and even elegance.

A Brief History of the Alphabet

The English language is a complex tapestry of extraordinary variety and colour. In order to appreciate how it has developed, we need to look at early British history and the ways in which successive invading forces exerted a powerful influence on the language.

When the Romans came to Britain in the mid-first century BC, they found a land inhabited – like much of Western Europe, including France and Germany – by various Celtic tribes, collectively known as Britons.

The Romans, under the command of Julius Caesar, invaded in AD 43, and brought with them their alphabet, formed from those of the Semitic, Egyptian Phoenician and Greek civilizations. The Latin alphabet consisted of twenty-three letters – our contemporary alphabet without the *j* (Julius was Iulius, and so on), *u* (the *v* – easier to carve in stone – was used for that sound) and *w* (see later).

By the end of the third century AD, most Romans had left Britain, which was now at the mercy of new invaders – Angles, Saxons and Jutes from Germany and Denmark. The Celts were driven away to the far-distant corners of Britain: Scotland, Ireland, Wales and Cornwall (where Celtic languages still survive to this day).

The invaders brought with them a runic alphabet and spoke a version of German that blended with the Celtic/Roman language already in existence in Britain to create Anglo-Saxon or Old English. In 597, however, Saint Augustine arrived in Kent on a mission from Pope Gregory to convert the people of Britain to Christianity. His success meant that, in order to read and study the Bible and other Christian texts in Latin, the Anglo-Saxons began to adopt the Roman alphabet, modifying it to suit their own requirements.

In 789 came the Viking invaders, and the English adopted many new words from the Old Norse: gap, ill, mire, reindeer, root, scowl, skull, sky, to mention a handful.

The Norman invasion of 1066 brought with it yet another influx of words. A two-tier language developed, with Norman French words being used by the ruling class, while their Anglo-Saxon equivalents were used by the natives. For this reason, we have a sheep or a cow (Anglo-Saxon) in the field but the more refined mutton or beef (from the French *mouton* and *bœuf*) at the table; the farmer's daughter wore a frock, but the lady of the manor wore a *robe*. Similarly, French tended to be used in law – thus we have words like mortgage (literally meaning 'dead pledge') or parole ('spoken word').

In the years following the Norman invasion, the last of the runic Old English letters gradually disappeared, replaced by letters from the Latin alphabet. Old English

common sheep   refined mutton

had given way to Middle English. During this period the three final letters joined the alphabet as we know it today: *j* was adapted from *i* when sounded as a consonant similar to a soft *g*; *v* as a consonant came to be distinguished from the vowel *u*; and *w*, with its similar sound, came into being as double-*u* (although the upper case form actually appears as double-*v*). The modern alphabet was complete.

The Nuts and Bolts, or Parts of Speech

Nouns: Naming Words

Nouns, as we know from school, are naming words. Things, people, places, chemical elements, music, concepts, emotions – all these are nouns. They form the majority of the words learned by a baby – nouns come first, then a few verbs are thrown in.

You may not need to be reminded, then, that they are usually divided into two main categories: **proper nouns** and **common nouns**. Common nouns are generic: 'planet', for instance, is a common noun – it could be one of many planets – but 'Jupiter', a proper noun, gives us a specific planet.

Proper nouns usually refer to people, places or titles. They tend to start with a capital letter and stand alone, without an 'a', 'an' or 'the'. Examples of proper nouns are

John, Paris, Mrs Jones, Friday and Jupiter; if you were telling someone about your mother, you could either refer to her as 'my mother' (common noun, even though she is a specific mother) or 'Mother' (proper noun) – you could equally refer to 'my dad' and 'Dad', and so on. Historical periods and events (the Stone Age, the First World War), the titles of natural phenomena (Hurricane Charlie) and specific geographical regions (the South of France) are all proper nouns.

Proper Plurals

Proper nouns are not usually referred to in the plural, but if you have three friends called Emma, you might refer to them as 'the (three) Emmas'; there are at least twelve Parises in the world, most of them in the US, not to mention Londons and even Berlins.

You might also say: 'I saw the Monets in the Louvre' – talking not about the man himself and his family but about his paintings. Similarly: 'Have you read any of the P. D. Jameses I lent you?'

Singular and Plural

Unlike proper nouns, common nouns, however, take plurals day in and day out, so we really need to know how to turn a singular into a plural.

The general rule for turning one into many is to add an *s* to the end of the word. Simples! Here are some examples (well there's one already):

book – books
computer – computers
table – tables

19

Nouns ending in a *y* after a consonant lose their final letter and replace it with *ies*:

> **baby – babies**
> **dictionary – dictionaries**
> **fairy – fairies**

Nouns ending in a *y* after a vowel are a different matter, however: they conform to the original rule of adding an *s*:

> **play – plays**
> **key – keys**
> **donkey – donkeys**

Most words that already end in *s* take *es* in the plural as do words ending with the similar-sounding *sh* and *ch*:

> **class – classes**
> **latch – latches**
> **waltz – waltzes**

Some nouns ending in *f* or *fe* change the f to a v and add *es*:

> **calf – calves**
> **knife – knives**
> **loaf – loaves**

But some nouns ending in f or *fe* simply add *s*:

chief – chiefs
cliff – cliffs
roof – roofs

When turning a singular into a plural, we must be careful to pluralize the correct part of the noun. For example, *mother-in-law* becomes *mothers-in-law* not *mother-in-laws* because it is the mothers who are the noun. The 'in-law' part of the word is descriptive and does not change. Along similar lines we have *man-at-arms* which becomes *men-at-arms*.

Some nouns remain the same whether they are being used in the singular or in the plural: deer, fish, jeans, scissors, sheep, species, wheat, and so on; *fishes* is also accepted as a plural and is nowadays usually used to refer to a number of different species. In order to distinguish between singular and plural with these nouns and a great many more like them, we must decide according to the context in which they are used.

There is another group of nouns (actually it is a subgroup of common nouns) known as non-count, uncountable or mass nouns which do not take a singular *or* a plural. They cannot be measured by number. Examples of these include water, evidence, happiness, rice and so on. In order to give a quantity for these we have to say *much*, *some*, *a lot of*, *a cupful* (then we worry if we should say 'two cupsful' or 'two cupfuls'. Despite the mothers-in-law above, the latter is actually correct and is proper common usage).

Abstract or Concrete?

There is little you imagine that is more concrete than, well, concrete. It is so solid that it holds together our buildings and cities. Think of concrete and you cannot fail to understand the difference between concrete nouns and the other kind – abstract. Concrete nouns are the names we give to things we can see, feel, hear, touch, smell: trees, elephants, cake *and* books, *to name but four.*

Examples of abstract nouns include tomorrow, thought, welfare, delight, belief, *etc. They tend to be non-countable, but there are a few exceptions such as music and structure; concrete nouns may or may not be countable: some rice (non-countable), three kittens (countable).*

Foreign Plurals

Singular	Plural	Origin
alga	algae	Latin
automaton	automata	Greek
criterion	criteria	Greek
gâteau	gâteaux	French
index	indexes/indices	Latin
kibbutz	kibbutzim/kibbutzes	Hebrew
phenomenon	phenomena	Greek
stimulus	stimuli/stimuluses	Latin

Irregular Nouns

No discussion of English plurals would be complete without the group of nouns that are a law unto themselves. They are known as irregular nouns. That is to say, in order to get them right, we simply have to know them. Luckily, they are commonly used and we tend to pluralize them automatically with very few problems. They are:

Singular	Plural
child	children
foot	feet
goose	geese
man/woman	men/women
mouse	mice
tooth	teeth

One more thing to be careful of is the noun *hair*. We always use this in the singular when referring to, say, 'a glorious head of hair', but it becomes plural if we are talking about a small number. So we would say 'my grandfather has a few grey hairs now'.

A Last Word on Nouns

Today, there is definitely something funny happening to some of our nouns. We seem to be forgetting what they are. Sometimes we turn one into an adjective and then add

Foreign Nouns

English has borrowed, on a long-term basis, an enormous number of words from foreign languages. We have kept-hold of the tendency to add English endings to all words, whether or not that is correct. Paparazzi *is already a plural in Italian (the singular would be* paparazzo*) so we should avoid the temptation to refer to* paparazzis*. On the other hand, you will attract some funny looks in Britain if you ask for two* cappuccini *or complain about a* graffito*. We seem to have accepted that two* cappuccinos *is the order of the day. We have to balance getting it right so as not to appear ignorant and avoid seeming pretentious.*

the noun ending on to that. For example, take the word *mist*. Occasionally, perhaps due to changing environmental conditions, *mist* becomes *mistiness*. Someone at the weather centre has taken a nice, short one-syllable noun and turned it first into an adjective – *misty* – then turned that back into a noun – *mistiness*. From time to time this is accompanied by *fogginess* in higher regions. Wait for outbreaks of *sunniness* or *snowiness* after dark.

Or, if we are not turning nouns into nouns-via-adjectives, we are using them as verbs. Traditionally nouns have been turned into verbs by the addition of a suffix to the noun or to its root word: *-ate*, *-en*, *-ify* or *-ize*, as in *captivate*, *frighten*, *liquefy*, *patronize*. But now, increasingly, any attempt at a suffix is dropped. Workers today are *tasked* to do something instead of being given a task (or even *asked* to do it). We now chair (or table something at) a meeting, torch a building or plate a meal. This usage can add colour or humour to what a person is saying – but it has to be deliberate and discerning. Indiscriminate use smacks of idleness.

Verbs: Doing Words

Verbs are sometimes known as 'doing' words or 'action' words – even if not much activity is visible; the point to bear in mind is that a verb tells us that someone or something is doing something.

Verbs are the most complex parts of speech. This is because, as well as describing an action, they tell us when the action took place, and give an indication as to who performed the action.

The Tenses: Verb Behaviour

The good news is that in this respect the English language is simpler than, say, French or German in that there are fewer verb endings to worry about. The **infinitive**, however, is a bit of an oddity in the English language. This is the purest form of the verb, without tense or person (see below), so its form does not change. Most infinitives in other languages are one word, but English infinitives take a *to* before the verb – *to be*, *to go*. This is why it's the only language that can split its infinitives – by inserting an adverb between *to* and the verb as in 'to boldly go'– much to the dismay of some purists, who point out that although the infinitive is made up of two words, those two words represent a single idea.

The **tense** tells us about the time of the action (now, in the past, in the future). The **person** refers to who is carrying out the action: **first person singular** (I); **second person singular** (you/thou); **third person singular** (he, she, it); **first person plural** (we); **second person plural** (you plural); and **third person plural** (they).

The grammatical term for the changes undergone by the verb relative to person and time (*I walk / I walked*; *he walks / he walked*, etc.) is **conjugation** (much more familiar in, for example, the French language – or Latin), while the changes to the verb (*walk / walks / walked*) are called **inflection.**

The Present Tense

The Simple Present

This is the Simple Present tense of *to walk*:

I walk	We walk
You walk	You (plural) walk
He/she/it walks	They walk

It is worth noting that the verb changes only for the third person singular.

The Simple Present tends to be used in general statements or to state attitudes, as in 'Koalas live in trees' or 'I don't trust politicians.'

The Present Progressive

This, also known as the Present Continuous, requires the **present participle**, which is the verb in its infinitive form, *walk*, with *-ing* on the end.

When the verb is in this form, it requires the **auxiliary verb** *to be* to accompany it; the other verb ending remains unchanged – 'walking':

I *am* walking	We *are* walking
You *are* walking	You *are* walking
He/she/it *is* walking	They *are* walking

This tense is used for actions that are current but not permanent or regular: 'Sally is sitting at her desk'; 'It is raining.'

Or, confusingly, it may refer to an action in the future: 'I am going there tomorrow'; 'We are flying to Spain next month.'

The Present Perfect

This requires the auxiliary verb *to have*, and the main verb ending (the Simple Past form, *walked*) remains the same.

I have walked	We have walked
You have walked	You have walked
He/she/it has walked	They have walked

This tense is used for an action that took place at some non-specified time. You do not say 'I have walked there last Monday,' for instance. You might say, 'I have never walked there' or 'I have walked there once.' The action referred to is in the past, but as seen from the present.

The Present Perfect Progressive

Also known as the Present Perfect Continuous, as its name suggests, this tense combines the Perfect and Progressive.

I have been walking, etc.

It is used to describe something that started in the past and is ongoing, as in 'I have been walking for hours and have still not reached the mountain.'

The Past Tense

Simple Past Tense

I walked	We walked
You walked	You walked
He/she/it walked	They walked

This tense is used for an action that took place at a specific time: 'I walked there this morning.'

The Past Progressive

Also known as Past Continuous, this tense follows the same pattern as the Present Progressive:

I was walking	We were walking
You were walking	You were walking
He/she/it was walking	They were walking

It is used to describe a longer action that was taking place in the past, where a shorter action interrupted it: 'I was walking to the park when it started to rain'; 'I was walking home when I remembered my appointment.' The 'interruption' is in the simple past.

The Past Perfect

This tense follows the pattern of the Present Perfect:

I had walked, etc.

For example: 'I had walked there once, but found it too far.'

The Past Perfect Progressive

This follows the pattern of the Present Perfect Progressive, except that all the 'action' is set in the past:

I had been walking, etc.

For example: 'I had been walking for hours and still had not reached the mountain when it began to rain.'

Irregular Verbs

These are verbs that, while they follow the general tense rules, have inflections – changes to their form – that do not conform. Two common examples are *to be* and *to go*.

Simple Present and Past Tense

I am/ was	**I go/went**
You are/were	**You go/went**
He/she/it is/was	**He/she/it goes/went**
We are/were	**We go/went**
You are/were	**You go/went**
They are/were	**They go/went**

Present and Past Progressive

I am going/I was going, and so on.

The Present Perfect

I have been/I have gone, and so on.

The Past Perfect

I had been/I had gone, and so on.

The Past Perfect Progressive

I had been being/I had been going.

Participles

These are forms of verbs that combine with the auxiliary verb to form the Perfect tense. In the examples above, the Present Participles are 'walking', 'being' and 'going'; and the Past Participles are 'walked', 'been' and 'gone'.

Participle Abuse

When using the verbs 'sit' and 'stand', in particular, it has become commonplace to use the Past Participle instead of the Present Participle. Thus people might say 'I **was sat** on the bus when it began to snow', *or* 'He **was stood** watching the carnival' – *this form is only correct if the passive voice is being used – i.e. as if somebody had placed 'me' in a seated position in the bus, or had placed the man in a standing position as though we were children or toys.*

Correctly phrased, these examples would use the present participle: 'I **was sitting** in the bus when it began to snow' *and* 'The man **was standing** watching the carnival' *(in such constructions you cannot avoid the repeated '-ing').*

The Present Participle can also be used as a noun denoting the action of a verb – '*Walking* is good for you.'

It can also be used be used as part of a verb – 'She was *walking* down the street.'

Or as an adjective – 'The *walking* man disappeared round the corner.'

The Past Participle can be used to form the passive voice: 'The burglar was *walked* to the police station'; and as an adjective: 'That is a well-*walked* dog.'

The Future Tenses

There are many ways in which we might talk of future events.

We might use the Present tense: 'The train *leaves* at 11 a.m. tomorrow.'

We can insert *will, shall* (usually limited to first person, singular or plural), or *going to*: 'He *will give* a talk at next week's conference'; 'I *shall go* there tomorrow'; 'We are *going to play* cards on Saturday.'

The Future Progressive tense can be the Present Progressive recycled. It is often used in discussing plans or arranged actions: 'I *am going* there next week'; 'They *are visiting* us in August'; 'What *are you doing* next week?'

Or *will be, shall be*, or *going to be* might be inserted: 'He *will be going* there next week'; 'I *shall be flying* to Australia tomorrow'; 'I'm *going to be clearing* the house on Saturday.'

We can use the Present Perfect Simple form (with *will*): 'On Monday I *will have had* the dog for three weeks.'

We can use the Present Perfect Progressive form (with

will): 'By the end of next month they *will have been married* for six years.'

And so on …

Adjectives and Adverbs: Describing Words

What is an Adjective?

Adjectives describe or give information about nouns and pronouns. The information might relate to:

How many or how much: *sixteen, five hundred, a few*, etc. (but see **Determiners**, p. 54)

Qualitative: colour, size, appearance, attributes of behaviour, etc.: *blue, large, sunny, bad-tempered, slow, gloomy, kind*

Possessive: *My, her, your, their* (these are **determiners** as well)

Demonstrative: *this, that, these, those* (also **pronouns, determiners**).

They can precede a noun in a sentence and qualify it, or give us details as to what it is like. This is called the **attributive** function: 'The *tall* tree'; 'The *yellow* ball'.

Alternatively, adjectives can stand away from their noun in a sentence, in which case there must be a verb present: 'The tree is *tall*'; 'The ball is *yellow*.'

Adjectives can be necessary when you need to be specific: 'Please pass me the *blue* book' – not the red one or the black one; 'Take the *right-hand* turn' – you could get lost otherwise; 'Exam candidates have *two* hours in which to complete this paper' – so get going.

Or they help the listener or reader to understand or visualize something: 'The dog was *savage*'; 'It was a *glorious* day.'

Adjectives distinguish one noun from another. They tell us that we are not talking about any old Christmas but a

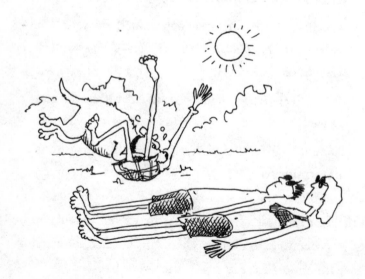

white one; a Christmas that is special because the snow is on the ground, in which the world looks *magical* and anything we wish for can come *true*. They are a part of speech that sets the imagination working by creating pictures in our minds.

Simile and Metaphor

Both of these devices are used to describe an object by associating or comparing it to something completely different.

A **metaphor** *often, but not always, employs the verb 'to be', such as 'a good book is a constant friend'. These phrases also contain metaphor: 'relations were starting to thaw' (comparing the relations to ice), 'the salesman landed the contract' (comparing the salesman to a fisherman and the contract to the fish) and 'he had a velvet voice' (comparing a sound to a texture).* **Similes** *are more straightforward and easier to spot, as they always use the words 'like' and 'as': 'Jim danced to the music like a wave on the sea' or 'Under her wig, Irene was as bald as a billiard ball'.*

Adjectives give us food that can be *scrumptious, comforting, delicious, nutritious, processed, fresh, sour, hot, heavy, indigestible* or *inedible*. They tell us whether books are *compelling, unreadable, derivative, unputdownable, boring* or *thrilling*.

Good writing entails choosing the appropriate word and tone for the occasion. Use adjectives when they add something to what you are saying. Do not over-use them – a good rule in writing or speaking English is to keep it clear and simple first and foremost – add the extras, such as adjectives and adverbs, only where they serve to enhance what you have said or written.

Comparative Adjectives: For Better or for Worse

You might find yourself comparing two things or people – and for that we use **comparative** adjectives. To form the comparative, we usually add *-er* to the end of an adjective (or *-r* if the adjective ends in *e*): 'Ben is *taller* than Bill'; 'The Mississippi is *wider* than the Seine.'

An exception to this is *far* – which becomes *farther* or *further*.

If the adjective has one syllable, with one vowel and one consonant at the end, double the consonant and add *-er*: *fat/*

fatter; *wet*/*wetter*. 'That is the *lesser* of our two problems.'

If the adjective is a word of two syllables ending in *y*, change the *y* to *i* and add *er*: *happy*/*happier*; *ugly*/*uglier*.

With longer adjectives, just add 'more' in front of it: '*more* boring'.

The exceptions are *good* and *bad*, which become *better* and *worse*.

With comparatives the word *than* is usually inserted after the adjective: 'Your dog is uglier *than* mine.'

There are exceptions, however. We might say 'Of the two dogs, yours is the *uglier*'; or 'Bill is tall, but Ben is *taller*.'

If you are comparing two people you always use the comparative. 'Bill and Ben are brothers – Bill is the *older* brother' – (or you can say 'Bill is the *elder*') **not** the *oldest* (or the *eldest*). (But you cannot say 'Bill is *elder* than Ben.') However, if they have a sister younger than Bill, then Bill can be termed the *oldest* of the three children.

Similarly, 'Of those two essays, yours is the *worse*'; but 'Of those three essays, yours is the *worst*.' (Oh, dear.)

Superlative Adjectives: The Best, the Worst and the Ugliest

We use the **superlative** when comparing more than two. To form the superlative, *-est* or *-st* is added where we would add *-er* or *-r* to form the comparative: 'Ben is the *tallest* of the three'; 'The Amazon is the *widest* river in the world.'

The superlative of those individualists *good* and *bad* are *best* and *worst*. Joining them is the superlative of *less* – *least*: 'That is the *least* of my many problems.'

The pattern follows that of the comparative: *fatter/fattest*; *wetter/wettest*.

In longer adjectives, *more* is replaced by *most*: *most boring*.

As a rule, the article *the* is inserted before the superlative: 'It is *the wettest* place on earth'; 'He chose to go to *the furthest* country he could find'; 'That is *the ugliest* dog I have ever seen'; 'That is *the most boring* speech he's ever given'; 'We get *the best* pupils here, and *the worst*.'

What is an Adverb?

Adverbs are to verbs what adjectives are to nouns. They tell us how verbs have been carried out. They usually describe actions, and they are very often formed by adding *-ly* to an adjective, at least a qualitative one: *happily, playfully, sunnily, bad-temperedly, slowly, gloomily, kindly,* and so on. Note that if the adjective ends in *y,* that *y* becomes *i* – usually: there are exceptions, for instance, *shyly.*

There are other ways of turning nouns and adjectives into adverbs, although these are less common and do not adhere to the general rule: down*wards,* grammar-*wise,* old-*style,* etc.

Adverbs can also describe the **time** or **place** of actions: 'We will catch the London train *tomorrow*'; 'My teacher worked *far away.*'

Or they can modify **numerals** and **pronouns**: 'There were *almost* a hundred books on my reading list'; '*All* those buildings are to be demolished.'

Adverbs are quite often used to modify **adjectives**: 'She is *extremely* pretty'; 'I am *very* tired.'

Sometimes they modify other **adverbs**: 'You did *very* well.'

At other times, they take the form of phrases or clauses (clauses have verbs; see p. 70): 'We came back from holiday *very reluctantly indeed*' (adverbial phrase); 'We came back from holiday *in time to start school*' (adverbial clause).

An Adverbial Oddity

Be alert to the meaning of the adverb quite. *It can mean 'somewhat' or 'fairly' or it can mean 'very' or 'absolutely': 'He is* quite *nice' (no emphasis: means he's all right, nothing special); 'He sewed on the button* quite *well' (slight stress on* quite *and rising note on* well: *fairly well, surprisingly); 'This is* quite *gorgeous' (stress on* quite: *it is very lovely); 'He is* quite *the nicest man I've ever met' (stress on* quite: *he's very nice); 'Yes, quite' (even stresses: I completely agree); 'This is* quite *an improvement' (slight stress on* quite: *it's a lot better).*

And of course, stumbling fingers on the keyboard might render it quiet, *so be careful. It is a mistake quite easy to make – sshh, correct it quite quietly.*

The Placing of Adverbs

Adverbs can quite often be moved about within a sentence, to precede or to follow the verb or its object, and still make sense. For example: 'The team captain scored both goals *skilfully*'; or 'The team captain *skilfully* scored both goals.' (You could even say '*Skilfully*, the team captain scored both goals' though that might sound rather odd.)

You can say 'The rain fell *suddenly*'; or '*Suddenly* the rain fell.'

If the adverb is longer than three syllables, you might find that the sentence flows better if you put it directly after the verb. For example: 'The politician spoke *eloquently* at the meeting' rather than 'The politician *eloquently* spoke at the meeting' or 'The politician spoke at the meeting *eloquently*.' The second breaks no rules but sounds awkward, while the last separates the verb from the adverb to such a degree that the sense is all but lost. A construction of this kind should be avoided where possible.

In some cases the placing of an adverb can alter the sense of the sentence. As with the adverb *only*:

'I *only* kicked the dog once' – implication: I did not do anything worse than kick it.

'I kicked *only* the dog once' – implication: I did not kick any other animals.

'I kicked the dog once *only*' or 'I kicked the dog *only* once' – implication: I did not kick it twice.

Use your inner voice to guide you at times like this. Read what you have written – aloud if it helps – and the chances of making errors are greatly reduced.

Comparative Adverbs: Better and Worse

These show, generally speaking, what one thing or person does better or worse than another. When the adverb ends in *-ly*, we add *more* before it: *quickly/more quickly*; *reluctantly/more reluctantly*. You can also use *less*: 'You drove *less well* during the test than in the lessons.' It is more comforting than *worse*.

Somewhat confusingly, if the adverb has the same form as an adjective, *-er* is added to the end, as though it was an adjective: 'Amina ran fast but Carla ran *faster*.'

And the individualists? The comparative adverb associated with *good* becomes *better*; and that associated with *bad* becomes *worse*. The same as the adjectives.

George plays football *well* but Hassan plays *better*.

I did *badly* yesterday – but today I'm doing *worse*.

Superlative Adverbs: The Worst and the Best

When the adverb ends in *-ly*, the superlative is formed by adding *most* in front of it: 'The doctor stitched up the wound *most skilfully*.'

If the adverb has the same form as an adjective, *-est* is added to the end: 'Of the three athletes, Hans ran the *fastest*.'

And *good* and *bad*? They become *the best* and *the worst*. As for *less* – that becomes *the least*, as in 'Jo ran *the least* fast.'

Adjective or Adverb?

One of the mistakes that is often made, in speech more than in writing, is the confusing of adjectives with adverbs: 'You'll have to move quick *if you want to catch the train'*; 'He crept timid *through the city'*; 'You did good.'

'Move', 'crept' 'did' *are all verbs, but* 'quick', 'timid' *and* 'good' *are all adjectives. Adjectives apply to nouns, adverbs to verbs: so the above sentences are incorrect.*

Here are the **correct** *versions:* 'You'll have to move quickly *if you want to catch the train'*; 'He crept timidly *through the city'*; *and* 'You did well.'

Pronouns: His and Hers

Personal

A pronoun is a word that stands in for a noun – for instance, to indicate someone or something already mentioned.

The most commonly used pronouns where the pronoun is the **subject** of the verb (that is, the person or thing that carries out the action), are *I, you* (singular and plural), *he, she, it, we, they*, as in '*He* took down the book' (where the book is the object).

The most commonly used **object** pronouns are *me, you* (singular and plural), *him, her, us, them*, as in 'The large dog knocked *him* over.'

Possessive Personal Pronouns

These are *mine; yours* (singular and plural); *his; hers; ours; theirs*. As in, 'That hat is *mine*, not *yours*'; 'That white house is *theirs*.' *My, your, his, her* and *there are*, also possessive personal pronouns, are classed as **determiners** (see p. 54).

Proper Use of Personal Pronouns

In speech and writing, these are generally used so as not to have to repeat a name or noun over and over again. Check, however that your meaning is clear – a sentence like the following leaves no one any the wiser as to who anyone is or how many of them there are: '*And then* **she** *said to* **her** *that* **he** *had gone to see* **her** *but* **she** *was out so* **he** *went to* **his** *friend's house and* **he** *said that* **she** *was driving in* **his** *car to see* **her** *friend …*'

Reflexive Pronouns

These are used to indicate that somebody or something is doing something to or for *themselves*:

> We cooked *ourselves* a delicious supper.
> The dog scratched *himself*.
> The wobbly chair righted *itself*.

Other Pronouns

Indefinite Pronouns are for when we cannot be definite about the person or thing concerned:

> Is there *anything* in there?
> *Who*'s going to lead the trek?
> *Someone* has put mud on the carpet.
> *Many* are called, but *few* are chosen.

Interrogative Pronouns are sometimes called 'wh' words because they are listed as *who, whom, which* and *what*. They are used as questions and must be chosen according to their role in the sentence: subject, object, etc.

Who left those footprints on the floor? (Subject)
Whose are those suitcases in the hall? (Possessive)
Which path shall we take? (Object)
To whom shall we give these cakes? (Indirect object)

Demonstrative Pronouns are **determiners** (see p. 54) and are often used in speech when we can actually indicate the item or person in question, by pointing or some other means:

This is the dress I bought.
Those potatoes will never feed us all.
These are my brothers.

Relative Pronouns join one part of a sentence to another. If the first part of the sentence has a person as its subject, the pronoun is *who* (*whom* if a person is the object); if it is a common noun it takes *that* or *which*.

Jean was the person *who* led the expedition.
The expedition *that* I went on was not led by Jean.
Pietro joined the expedition in *which* I climbed the mountain.
He was the person *whom* I trusted to lead us.

In speech, *whom* is nowadays often dropped in favour of the simpler *who* – possibly because people are uncertain about its application or feel self-conscious about using it, but in written English it is still the accurate construction if you are being formal.

Little Parts of Speech ... All the Rest

Prepositions: Over, Under, Sideways, Down

Prepositions are words that express the relationship (temporal, spacial or otherwise) between a noun or pronoun and another element in the phrase.

In other words, a preposition tells us where (or when) something is in relation to something else. For example: 'The man *on* the platform'; or 'He arrived *after* dinner.'

There are over one hundred prepositions in English, but those occurring most frequently refer to time or place:

Time prepositions include: *before, after, during, at, by, for, since*

Place prepositions include: *under, over, on, off, through, down, around*

Up With It Put

It has been a matter of controversy for some time whether or not it is permissible to end a sentence with a preposition. Winston Churchill, whose mastery of the language was undeniable, demonstrated how clumsy that could make the language seem: 'This is the sort of English up with which I will not put.'

However, it is now generally considered that if you need to put a preposition at the end of a sentence, then go ahead and do so. If you apply common sense and your inner ear, you should not go wrong.

Sometimes prepositions are two or three words long: *Owing to, because of, off of, in spite of, with reference to, in accordance with, except for*, etc. These are more self-explanatory and their use is more specific, so it is easier to be confident of using the correct expression.

Many people are a bit uncertain as to what preposition to use – why for instance do we say 'I'll see you *on* Monday', but 'I'll see you *at* four o'clock' and 'I'll see you *at* the weekend'? (Indeed there is an increasing tendency – possibly under the influence of US English – to say '*on* the weekend'.) When in doubt, consult a good dictionary or a book on English grammar.

This, That and the Other: Determiners

Determiners are similar to pronouns and adjectives in that they give information about nouns. Rather than describe nouns, they specify them. Some adjectives and pronouns are determiners, as are the **Definite** and **Indefinite Articles** (*the, a, an*).

Unlike adjectives and possessive pronouns, however, they can never be separated from the nouns to which they belong. '*My* book'; '*Our* house'; '*The* dog'; '*That* man'; etc.

Other determiners include:

Demonstratives: *this, that, these, those, yonder*

Indefinite determiners: *some, few, less, several, many, much, neither*, etc.

Numbers: cardinal and ordinal: i.e. *one* or *the first*

Definite and Indefinite: The Articles

The distinction between **definite** and **indefinite** is as the names suggest – *the* refers to a specific (definite) person or thing – we assume that the reader or listener already know which noun we are referring to: 'Mary took *the* dog for a walk'; '*The* house needs re-decorating.' If we replace *the* with *a*, we are talking about any (indefinite) dog and any house.

The use of **an** is determined by the first letter of the word that follows. Pronouncing two vowel sounds separately one after the other is awkward. To keep them distinct from each other we use **an** as in '*an* elephant' or '*an* understatement'. It is a more elegant solution than the glottal stop (a sound from the back of the throat as air is released) sometimes heard in parts of Britain: 'Pass me *a* apple.'

Similarly, *the* is lengthened to *thee* before a word beginning with a vowel: 'He is *thee* expert on Japanese painting'; '*Thee* umbrella is by the door.'

Both *a* and *the* can occasionally be lengthened (to *ay* and *thee*) for the purposes of emphasis. 'No, not *your* car – *ay* car'; 'It is *thee* finest wine.'

The Zero Article

Certain nouns require neither a definite nor an indefinite article. This is known as the zero *article. When nouns are used in this way, they allow us to generalize about them: 'Home is where the heart is'; 'Ink will stain your clothes'; 'Anger is a destructive emotion.'*

Conjunctions: Not Only, But Also

English contains two main forms of conjunctions or joining words: *coordinating conjunctions* and *subordinating conjunctions*.

Coordinating conjunctions join together parts of the sentence that have equal weight. The most commonly used of these is *and*: 'The Orient Express stopped at Strasbourg *and* Vienna *and* Budapest *and* Bucharest'; 'The boys came home hungry *and* tired *and* dirty.'

The list of items or adjectives that can be joined by *and* in this way is endless and each item will carry equal importance.

In similar situations we have *but* which suggests contrast and *or* which suggests choice: 'Cycling to work is better for your health, *but* getting the train is quicker'; 'I don't know whether to cycle *or* get the train this morning.'

Cycling and getting the train are equal, at least to the grammarian, in these sentences.

Subordinating conjunctions are a little more complex than coordinating conjunctions. They join together parts of the sentence that do not have equal weight; the second part being subordinate to the main part. For example: 'We will go for a walk *when* the snow has melted.'

The main bit is 'We will go for a walk'; 'the snow has melted' is subordinate to it, and the two are joined by the conjunction *when*.

The conjunctions you are most likely to come across are *although, and, because, but, if, or, so, unless, when* and *while*.

There is a traditionally held belief that it is wrong to begin a sentence with *And* or *But*. Perhaps some schools still maintain this rule, but no one has come up with a good reason for it. Obviously, if it is unnecessary, then it should be left out – but since the earliest times the best of writers have begin sentences with *And* and *But*, to their stylistic advantage. It is definitely a rule to be flouted. But judiciously.

When *And* Means *To*

And *is a connecting word – it connects words, numbers, phrases or sentences, and is sometimes used to introduce an additional comment. Roughly speaking, it means* also *or* as well.

But it is sometimes used in place of the word to *in an infinitive, as in 'We should go* and *buy a new alarm clock.' This should be 'We should go* to *buy a new alarm clock.'*

Why one simple word has been replaced by another is uncertain – perhaps because it was felt that the two verbs (in this case go *and* buy*) had to be joined by a conjunction. It is a construction that is common in colloquial speech but should be avoided in formal writing.*

Prefixes and Suffixes

One of the various ways in which many English words have been created is by affixation: that is the addition of prefixes, *which are attached to the beginning of a word, and* suffixes, *which are tagged on to the end. While some prefixes simply modify or adapt the meaning of the root word (*understaffed *or* outclassed, *for example), others may reverse the meaning completely. Take, for example,* disbelief, unfriendly *or* demystify. Dis-, un- *and* de- *are the three most commonly used prefixes that turn a positive word into a negative.*

One of the most common suffixes is -ise/ize, *which changes a noun to a verb:* real/realize *or* critic/criticize, *etc. The* -ly *suffix makes an adverb:* real/really; *-ity makes a noun from an adjective:* similar/similarity.

Making Sense of Sentences

If we are to express ourselves clearly and precisely in English, it is vital to understand and make use of the rules of grammar regarding sentence structure and word order – putting words in the right order is crucial to the sense of our speech and writing.

In the last chapter, most of the components of a sentence have been covered. Nouns, verbs, adjectives, adverbs, prepositions and conjunctions – all are put together to form phrases, clauses and sentences. A sentence may be defined as a unit of grammar that consists of a **subject** (a noun) and a **predicate** (which consists of at least a verb). Together they form a unit that expresses a complete thought or idea: 'The baby [subject] cried [verb].'

These are examples of simple sentences as they are complete in themselves. More complex sentences also contain an **object**. The object is sometimes described as the *victim*: the noun that is on the receiving end of the subject's action. For example: 'The child [subject] dropped [verb] the doll [object].'

The subject always comes first in sentence structure and the rest of the sentence (the predicate) gives us more information about the subject. If we were to place the subject in the position of the object and vice versa, the meaning of the sentence would be reversed. In the example above, the doll would have dropped the child. Wrong word order makes a nonsense of what we are trying to say.

In a very simple sentence, the verb follows the subject. If the verb is **intransitive** – that is to say, it does not require an object in order to make sense – the subject-verb format creates a complete sentence: 'The rain fell.' (Subject-verb.) If we use a **transitive** verb, one that requires an object, we need to bring in a third element to our simple sentence: 'Jennifer caught the measles.' (Subject-verb-object.) 'Jennifer caught' does not make sense without an object.

Very short sentences like these can sometimes have dramatic effect – 'Her heart broke' – but should be used judiciously. A string of very short sentences sounds stilted and more like a small child's first literacy exercises.

Word order is also related to the mood of a sentence, and to whether the statement is in the active or passive voice (see p. 65).

What is a Mood?

The word *mood* (sometimes *mode*) comes from the Latin *modus*, which means 'manner'. The verb's mood indicates the writer's or speaker's viewpoint.

The **indicative** mood is used in statements of fact: 'It is raining today'; 'My new car is blue.'

When we ask questions the mood is **interrogative** and

the subject *follows* the auxiliary verb ('has'): 'Has the baker sold out of bread?'

The **imperative** mood is used for commands: 'Go and get your bag'; 'Shut the door.'

The **subjunctive** is used for expressing hypothetical or unreal statements, wishes, suggesting, hopes, emphasizing urgency. Most of the time it goes unnoticed as only the verb 'to be' and the present tense third person singular (he/she/it) change, the former taking the forms *be* or *were*, and the latter losing the final *s* or *es*.

'I wish I *had* more time to paint'; 'I wish I *were* able to draw like that'; 'If she *were* less rude she would have more friends'; 'I suggest that he *come* at the weekend'; 'It is vital that you *be* at that meeting.'

If she were less rude she would have more friends.

Active and Passive: Do As You Would Be Done By

The Active Voice is when the **subject** of the sentence carries out the action. In the following sentence, the **subject** is the man, the **object** is the car.

The man washes his car.

Simple and straightforward. The subject is doing something to the object. In the Passive Voice, it is the subject that is at the receiving end. If we were to switch the sentence above to the Passive Voice, the subject changes (otherwise the car would be washing the man):

The car is washed by the man.

As this one shows, sentences in the Passive can often sound awkward and stilted. But in some cases it is useful – for instance, where the 'doer' is considered less important or less relevant than the 'done-to': 'That house has been repainted inside and out' or 'That house has been completely repainted by the landlord.'

Or when an action has been carried out by person or persons unknown: 'His bicycle was stolen'; 'The broken fence has been mended.'

Or to avoid blaming someone directly, or even admitting having done something yourself: 'The CDs were dropped on the floor' or 'Top-secret papers were mislaid.'

So, the passive can be useful and in some sentence constructions you might find it unavoidable. But do not over-use it – it can sound pompous or evasive. Remember you can always blame that person called Someone: 'Someone has dropped mud all over the floor'; 'Someone has mislaid top-secret papers.'

Simple, Complex and Compound Sentences

Let's deal with the differenct types of sentence in order of complexity.

Simple Sentences

We have seen that simple, declarative sentences follow a fixed word order: **subject**, **verb** and **object**. In many cases that is followed by the **indirect object**. This applies in all cases except when we employ a pronoun as our indirect object (*me*, *them*, *us*, etc.). Although the established sentence structure changes when we are asking a question, exclaiming or using the subjunctive mood, if we are making a statement, we must put words in this order:

Granny put the Christmas present on the table.
(subject-verb-object-indirect object)

The exception to this rule of word order applies when we replace the noun with a pronoun in talking about the **indirect object**. If the present were given *to me* and the sentence can be re-worked so that the pronoun (*me*) is the recipient of something, *I* am the indirect object and the word order changes accordingly.

Granny gave *me* the Christmas present.

The word order has now become **subject**, **verb**, **indirect object** (*me*), **object**. If it is possible to re-phrase the original sentence so that the object (*me*) takes a preposition such as *to, by, with* or *from*, for example, it is an indirect object.

Granny gave the Christmas present to me.

Complex Sentences

These, you will not be surprised to learn, are more complicated than simple sentences. They contain additional information in the form of **subordinate clauses**. If we take our first sentence about Granny and add a conjunction (or joining word) to it, we see that it becomes incomplete:

> *Although* Granny put the Christmas present on the table…

It has moved from a simple sentence to an unfinished fragment and needs further information to make it complete. Let's add some more details and have another look:

> Although Granny put the Christmas present on the table, she had forgotten to wrap it.

That now makes sense as a complete, complex sentence. Our initial sentence ('Granny put the present on the table') has become a **subordinate clause** and our additional information a **main clause**. The two are joined together by the conjunction *although*.

Subordinating conjunctions join subordinate clauses to main clauses. Examples include *unless*, *since*, *whereas*, *while*, *if* and *after*.

Compound Sentences

Complex sentences, as we have seen, contain a subordinating (or dependent) clause that will not stand up on its own, and a main (or independent) clause that will. In **compound sentences**, however, we have clauses of equal weight, all of them independent (that is to say making sense on their own), joined by a conjunction, usually *and*, *but* or *or*. An example of this is:

I'll take the high road, **but** you'll take the low road.

Because the two parts are independent, this could just as well be written in two complete simple sentences:

I'll take the high road. You'll take the low road.

Some compound sentences have more than two clauses of equal weight.

The way to distinguish between complex and compound sentences is that complex sentences contain **conjunctive adverbs** that tell us the relationship between one clause and the next:

They agreed, however, that the introduction of Tom to his new office and office companions could hardly fail to throw a light upon the subject; and **therefore** postponed its further consideration until after the fulfilment of the appointment they had made with Mr Fips.

—Charles Dickens, *Martin Chuzzlewit*

His looks and words meant more to her than other men's, **because** she cared more for them.

—George Eliot, *Middlemarch*

There are a great many conjunctive adverbs that can be found in complex sentences. Some relate to time: *at last, finally, later, next*, etc. Others give a contrast: *instead, otherwise, on the contrary, on the other hand*, etc. Some allow us to reach a conclusion: *thus, finally, similarly, in addition*, etc. Any clause introduced by one of these will be a subordinate clause, dependent on a main clause for its meaning.

Clauses and Phrases

A complex sentence can be broken down into groups of words called clauses and phrases.

Clauses

If a sentence is the most important and most complete unit of grammar, the next in importance is the clause. Sentences are made up of clauses, but a clause will not necessarily make sense on its own (although a simple sentence may consist of nothing but a clause): its purpose is usually to add information about the subject of a sentence. In order to be defined as a clause, the information must contain a verb.

Not all clauses are created equal. We have main clauses, which make sense on their own, and subordinate clauses, which do not. Subordinate clauses may be divided up even further into four different types: *noun, adverbial, relative* or *comparative.*

Phrases

A phrase is either a single word or a group of words without a verb (unless it is a verbal phrase) and does not make sense on its own. It does not fit the subject-predicate structure the way that a clause does; instead it is analysed according to its main word and the words that modify it. Phrases can be *adjectival, adverbial, noun, verbal* or *prepositional.*

Let us look at some individual phrases:

When you see Sibyl Vane [*adverbial phrase*] you will feel [*verbal phrase*] that the man who could wrong her [*noun phrase*] would be [*verbal phrase*] a beast [*noun phrase*], a beast without a heart [*adjectival phrase*].

—Oscar Wilde, *The Picture of Dorian Gray*

A stream [*noun phrase*], unseen but clamorous [*adjectival phrase*], fell echoing down [*verbal phrase*] close at hand [*adverbial phrase*].

—Dorothy L. Sayers, *Hangman's Holiday*

Phrases, as we can see, can be separated off from the main sentence by commas. When we do this, it makes the sentence easier to read as we are given a slight pause between the basic information and the subsidiary details.

Word order is still vitally important if we are to make sense. Phrases should be placed as close as possible to the word to which they add information.

The Seven Stages of Sentences

There are seven ways of breaking down sentences into their basic clause types. If we refer to each element by its initial we have:

S = *subject*, V = *verb*, O = *object*, C = *complement*
and A = *adverbial/adjectival*.

Using these elements we have the following combinations available:

S + V (intransitive verb):   'The dog barked.'

S + V + O (transitive):   'The dog saw the postman.'

S + V + C: 'The dog is an Alsatian.'

S + V + A: 'The dog barks loudly.'

S + V + O + O: 'The dog gave me a bite.'

S + V + O + C: 'The dog got its paws wet.'

S + V + O + A: 'The dog bit the postman on his ankle.'

These are the magnificent seven. If any element were to be changed or omitted, the sense would be lost. While some rearrangement is possible, this structure is the basic framework of all sentences.

The Complement

A word about the complement. *While most verbs are followed by objects and indirect objects, there is an exception. Luckily, it is one of those exceptions that occurs so frequently that we are familiar with it already, whether we realize it or not. The verb* to be *– and similar verbs such as* become, seem *etc. – take not an object but a complement. This means that the subject and what is said about it are the same thing. For example:*

She is a sculptor.

The stew tasted of caraway.

The verbs in these cases are called copulative *verbs, which makes sense given that their job is to unite the two parts of the sentence: the subject and what is said about them. The complement in these cases may be a noun, pronoun, adverb or adjective in any form.*

Signposts, or Why Punctuation Matters

Writing without punctuation has been compared to driving without road signs. Without it, we would be utterly lost, travelling at the wrong speed in the wrong direction and irritating everyone around us. Read any unpunctuated paragraph and you will feel compelled to agree. Punctuation is vital because it tells us, among other things, when to stop, when to have a short breather and when we are moving from one thought to the next. If we are asking a question we need punctuation to let others know we are asking. We might be exclaiming or expressing urgency or surprise; again, punctuation tells us that this is so. It also indicates to us what belongs to whom (in the form of apostrophes) and alerts us to the fact that letters have been removed or words run together. And it tells us whose words are which – or which words are whose.

Incorrect punctuation can completely alter the sense of what we are writing.

Take the following phrases:

> Bring me the ball boy
> Ladies clearance sale
> The boy's like chocolate
> Thirty minute meals
> Fifty odd hats
> Do not pull emergency brake

If we re-punctuate them, we find a completely different meaning for each of them:

> Bring me the ball, boy
> Ladies' clearance sale
> The boys like chocolate
> Thirty-minute meals
> Fifty-odd hats
> Do not pull. Emergency brake

Even if we feel that punctuation is too troublesome and not worth the headache, we must think of our readers: it is a courtesy to them to let them know how we would like our text to be read. It

shows them the respect they are due to put our thoughts in a good, coherent order; to finish one idea before embarking on the next and to show where one thought ends and the next one begins.

It shows whether we are making a statement or asking a question; whether we are quoting someone else or expressing our own thoughts. Readers need guidance, much more than people we are talking to face to face, where tone of voice, even facial expressions, show us the speaker's meaning. Much of that guidance comes through good punctuation.

The Full Stop or Full Point: You Have a Point

The full stop is the most basic punctuation mark and something we all remember from our earliest days at school.

John sees the ball.

Janet plays with the dog.

Remember? Every sentence ends with a full stop – exclamation marks and question marks incorporate full points – and begins with a capital letter.

A full stop (known as a *period* in the United States) marks the end of a particular thought or idea and tells the reader to pause and prepare for the next one. Music without rests would have no rhythm or mood; the silence is as important as the sound. The same applies to written English and the full stop. When you are reading aloud, the full stop marks a point in the text where you can draw breath before moving on.

When writing two separate statements, it is usually necessary to use a full stop between them. A comma is not adequate. For example: 'Janet planted roses in her garden, she's thinking of planting more next year.'

A comma does not allow enough pause to keep the two thoughts apart; a full stop is required: 'Janet planted roses in her garden. She's thinking of planting more next year.'

Or you could pop in an *and* in place of the full stop to run the two ideas together to make the sound more fluent: 'Janet planted roses in her garden and she's thinking of planting more next year.'

If in doubt, read your sentences aloud. If the rhythm feels wrong, adjust the punctuation until you are happy with the way it sounds.

Three (and it has to be three, no more and no fewer) evenly spaced full stops together have a use of their own. Known as an ellipsis, the dots indicate omitted words, either because they are of no relevance, or because you'd rather not: 'A terrifically … exciting film,' a poster might quote from a review – omitting the words 'boring remake of an'.

Or the ellipsis may be to indicate that for some reason the sentence is falling away. Perhaps the speaker is losing the power to talk: 'I hereby bequeath my worldly goods to my darling…'

It is a very useful tool if you wish to give the impression that something interesting is about to take place but you are, for some reason, unable to say what that might be. It is, therefore, beloved of blurb writers who might write something like:

> When a second body is found in a nearby forest, the forensic team draw their own conclusions…

In *The Power and the Glory*, Graham Greene's use of ellipses gives a powerful impression that there are a great many things that must remain unspoken:

> It's been so long…
> Say an Act of Contrition for your sins. You must trust God, my dear, to make allowances…
> I wouldn't mind suffering…

If you re-read this short passage replacing the ellipses with simple full stops the sense of yearning and loss is destroyed. Those two extra dots have an enormous emotional power.

The Comma: Pause for Thought

While the application of the comma is hotly debated, it seems to have gone out of fashion to some degree in recent decades. If you read a Victorian novel, you will find it is heavily punctuated, a blizzard of commas, semi-colons and colons; whereas recent fiction is more sparing in its comma use. The point is not to follow fashion, however, but to use a comma when it is sensible to use it and to do away with it otherwise.

The comma has a great many applications. Whereas the full stop, the exclamation mark and the question mark have rules to be followed, there is less that is written in stone when it comes to the comma. This, however, gives the writer greater scope to misapply it. Skilfully employed, the comma allows the reader to put the appropriate breaks in a text and to understand clearly what the writer is saying. When misused, the comma can turn the meaning back to front; sometimes it can simply confuse and bewilder.

Compare: 'I picked all the flowers, which were growing over the path.'

With: 'I picked all the flowers which were growing over the path.'

In the first sentence, *all* the flowers were growing over

the path. In the second, I picked only those that were growing over the path; I left the rest unpicked.

Compare also: 'The man said his wife was crazy.'

With: 'The man, said his wife, was crazy.'

When we bracket off the *said his wife*, we are left with a totally opposite meaning.

Having witnessed the power of the comma to alter the sense of what we are saying, let's have a look at its many uses.

1. The comma should be used to separate items in a list: 'That weekend we watched *Shrek*, *Toy Story* and *Alice in Wonderland*.'

    Normally we would *not* use a comma after the penultimate item on the list. The word *and* acts as the comma break and leads the reader to the final item. If, however, there is any ambiguity, for example if the last item consists of two names, a comma clarifies the sense: 'That weekend we watched *Manhattan*, *Annie Hall*, and *Hannah and Her Sisters*.'

2. The comma is used before direct speech. If you are writing dialogue, you always need to put a comma before your quotation marks to separate the part of the text that is written from that which is spoken. For example: 'Sally turned round and said, "I'd love a cup of coffee."'

3. Commas are used in a similar way to brackets – to separate a secondary idea in a sentence from its main thrust. In this case, commas **must** bring a partner, as a single comma has no virtue on its own. It leaves the reader wondering at what point the aside ends and the sentence returns to its main idea:

> She walked slowly, having broken the heel of her shoe, as she crossed the bridge that night.

> The ship was bound for New York, not Boston as I had believed, and was due to depart the following week.

In these cases, the words within the commas can be removed entirely and the sentence will still make perfect sense.

We often bracket off names in sentences with the use of two commas. When the something or someone discussed is the only one of its kind, it should be set off by commas. If not, not. The following example gives some importance to the wife's name:

> The Mayor and his wife, Eleanor, attended a banquet at the Guildhall.

However, to say 'The Mayor and his wife Eleanor attended a banquet at the Guildhall' is not wrong – even though there is a faint suggestion that he might have a 'wife

Anna' and a 'wife Charlotte', and maybe others hidden away somewhere.

There is a subtle difference too between the two following statements:

> The Beatles' album *Let it Be* sold millions of copies.
>
> The Beatles' final album, *Let it Be*, sold millions of copies.

In the first sentence, the album we are referring to is one of many (non-defining) and so it does not require the commas. In the second sentence, we have specified the album as being their last and so it becomes necessary to put the title within commas. If we removed the title (the words between the commas) in the second sentence, it would still make sense: we cannot do this to the first without it losing its meaning.

If you find that when you remove the material you have written within commas the sentence does not still hold together, the chances are that you have placed the commas incorrectly. Have another look and read aloud if necessary.

4. Commas after a word of introduction: if a sentence begins with an introductory word, perhaps an adverb of time such as *later*, *afterwards*, *before* or *a long time ago*,

that word or phrase should be followed by a comma. The short pause it allows the reader gives time for reflection and mentally setting the scene.

Before the war, I used to gather seashells on this beach.

One day, when the snow has melted, we should visit your mother.

This is also true in certain cases where we use the words *however*, *nevertheless* and *meanwhile*. Each sentence needs to be considered individually depending on usage. For example:

However you look at it, we still need to take a present with us.

However, if we do go to the party, we will need to take a present.

In the first the lack of comma gives 'however' the meaning of 'whichever way'; in the second, the comma gives it the meaning 'but'.

5. Commas around a name: if we are directly using a person's name, or form of address, we need to separate it from the rest of the sentence with commas.

> For Heaven's sake, Catherine, don't look so angry!
> —Linton in *Wuthering Heights*

> Pity, Jane, from some people is a noxious and insulting sort of tribute.
> —Mr Rochester in *Jane Eyre*

To omit commas here can be misleading and confusing – or sometimes hilarious:

For example, 'I'm drowning Mother!' should no doubt read 'I'm drowning, Mother!' and demonstrates the great importance of a single, tiny mark.

6. Commas for balance: if a sentence contains two contrasting ideas, the two can be set against each other with a comma. For example:

If not now, when?

I'll say what I think, not what I'm told.

She learned to play the violin, not the double bass.

Here is Jane Austen demonstrating in *Emma* how use of the comma gives her command of her prose and keeps her sentence gently bubbling along, without abrupt breaks or confusion:

> Emma Woodhouse, handsome, clever, and rich, with a comfortable home and happy disposition, seemed to unite some of the best blessings of existence; and had lived nearly twenty-one years in the world with very little to distress or vex her.

7. In calling, asking and exclaiming – more formally known as *vocative* and *interjective*, this use of the comma is easier than it sounds. If there is an exclamation, such as

oh good gracious! in a sentence it is necessary to surround it by commas for clarity. For example:

I believe I can see, oh good heavens, an oasis in the distance.

If you wish to end a sentence with a question, you also need to place a comma between the statement and the question to separate the two. For example:

You'll be home for dinner tonight, won't you?

8. The 'comma splice': when we examined the use of the full stop, we noted that a comma is sometimes incorrectly used in its place. This is known as the comma splice. For example:

> Mary went to the park yesterday, she saw several swans on the lake.

The use of the comma is incorrect here because the two ideas are separate. However, if we join them in this way, the comma is adequate for balancing the sentence and allows a slight pause before the second clause:

> *When* Mary went to the park yesterday, she saw several swans on the lake.

9. Commas may also be used to balance a sentence when the verb is written once, but applies to two different subjects. For example:

> Natalie wore a red dress, Melanie a green.
> Some people enjoy champagne, others prosecco.

In the first example the verb *wore* applies to both girls and its use is implied to both by the use of the comma. In the second, *enjoy* refers to some people and does not need to be repeated because the comma carries the meaning across.

The best advice anyone can give about the use of the comma is to read and re-read everything you have written with a critical mind. Use your inner ear to add pauses that follow a natural rhythm and, under no circumstances, apply the scattergun approach to punctuation that is all too common.

The Colon and Semicolon: Introducing a Longer Pause

Colons are used less frequently today than they were in the eighteenth and nineteenth centuries. Semicolons have to some extent taken their place as indicative of a pause somewhere between full stop and comma, often linking two related clauses. The main use of a colon today is to introduce a list, an example or an explanation. (This book is full of examples of the uses of a colon.) Here are two examples:

Here the colon introduces an explanation as to what is wanted:

What I want to know is this: ought I at once to take such steps as I can to discover the writer of the letter?

—Wilkie Collins, *The Woman in White*

Here the colon introduces a list of colourful skirts:

> The women's long cloth skirts are printed so gaily with
> the oddest things: there is no telling when a raft of
> yellow umbrellas, or the calico cat and the gingham
> dog, or an upside-down image of the Catholic Pope
> might just go sauntering across our yard.
>
> —Barbara Kingsolver, *The Poisonwood Bible*

The colon may also be used in place of a comma before a
speech in a play, to separate the name of the speaker from
the words spoken (and, of course, before an example):

Hamlet: To be, or not to be ...

Or to put two ideas in opposition: 'Finders keepers: losers
weepers'.

It may also be used to separate a main title from its
subtitle: *Twenty-First-Century Punctuation: The Demise of
the Colon*.

One technical point – you need a space after the colon,
but not before.

Open an English novel at any page and you can almost
guess its date according to the way it has been punctuated.
The Victorians enjoyed long sentences kept in order by
commas, semicolons, colons and dashes. Modern writers

seem to prefer shorter sentences, perhaps connected by conjunctions. This indicates that the semicolon is subject to fashion to some degree and, therefore, less likely to have hard and fast rules for its use.

The main purpose of the **semicolon** is to demonstrate a connection between two parts of a sentence and to hold the two parts together but to allow the reader a moment's breath between them. Sometimes conjunctions such as *nevertheless*, *however*, *consequently* and so on follow a semicolon:

> She wished to study literature; however, the course was full.

The semicolon may also be used to separate off complex points in a list:

> The hotel offered splendid accommodation: there was a gym with a treadmill, a rowing machine and weights; a lounge, a bar and a terrace restaurant; gardens, a pool and a hot tub.

There is a tendency nowadays to insert a semicolon where a colon is required. This is in part because many people are not familiar with the semicolon and its uses – and possibly because colon and semicolon share the same key on a keyboard.

Question? Exclamation!

There is one, and only one, important thing to remember about the **question mark**: use it only after a direct question. While this seems quite straightforward, it is often overlooked. To be sure that we know what we're doing, we need to differentiate between a direct and an indirect question. These are direct questions:

'When will the cake be ready?'

'Are you going to the dance on Sunday?'

When the question is indirect, the sentence takes the form of a statement and so it is quite correct to drop the question mark and use the full stop. For example:

'Yasmine wondered when the cake would be ready.'

'Rosa asked her sister what she was planning to wear to the dance.'

Sometimes, just the question mark is enough: 'She's going to the dance on Sunday?'

If we replace it with a full stop, the question becomes a statement: 'She's going to the dance on Sunday.'

The dictionary tells us that to exclaim is to cry out in surprise, anger, pain, etc. An **exclamation mark** indicates to the reader that a strong emotion lies behind the words.

It can transform a short phrase like *This is it* into an expression of awe, terror or amazement – *This is it!*

While used rather promiscuously today, the exclamation mark is irreplaceable in situations where it conveys a great sense of immediacy.

It can be used after a command: 'Run and fetch the doctor!'

After a warning: 'Never think of doing that again!'

To convey urgency: 'We need boiling water – now!'

To express strong emotion: 'May they always be happy!'

Surprise: 'No!'

It has also been said that the exclamation mark can be used to express scepticism. Such a use might take the form of:

He's working late again? Sure!

She's lost a stone already!

The exclamation mark may also be used to invoke someone or something. Sometimes it does this poetically: 'Oh my beloved!'

Sometimes a little more prosaically: 'Oi! Mister!'

In his *Modern English Usage*, Fowler tells us that we should avoid the exclamation mark when the sentence gives us the full emotion in the words alone. A sentence such as *That is a lie* gives us the meaning in full. It therefore only requires an exclamation mark if the tone in which it is said differs from what is written on the page.

Because the exclamation mark intensifies a sentence or a line of dialogue, there is a tendency to use it to beef up lack-lustre prose. This should be avoided where possible. If you find yourself resorting to too many exclamation marks, check what you have written and see if it can be improved in other ways. We will look at this and other stylistic problems in the final chapter. One word of warning: using more than one exclamation mark at a time can turn your writing into a comic book. Please use them advisedly. And sparingly.

The Apostrophe: Possession is Nine-Tenths of the Law

Despite its diminutive size, the apostrophe has managed to create havoc in written English. It seems that even academics, writers and editors cannot entirely agree on the proper use of the apostrophe in certain cases, while the rest of us can get pretty steamed up when we see signs abusing the poor apostrophe. We misuse the apostrophe in three main ways:

We put it in the wrong place.

We fail to use it where we should.

We put it where we don't need it.

If you need evidence of this, have a look at the website of the Apostrophe Protection Society, which has thousands of examples ranging from *Suttons Snax's* (I really don't know where to begin with this one) to *Beaver's use their teeth* and *crispy roast potato's*. Tragically, the list goes on and on …

Let's start with problem one, putting the apostrophe in the wrong place. That means we need to know where the right place is. Well, the apostrophe has two main uses: possession and contraction.

That's the editor; he's a stickler for apostrophes.

Possession

Singular

When we have a singular noun possessing something, the apostrophe follows the noun and is followed by an s:

Jennifer's diary (the diary of Jennifer)

the boy's life (the life of the boy).

This is true even if the noun already ends in an *s*: 'St James's Park'.

Plural

When we have a noun that goes into a regular plural, that is to say it has an *s* on the end, we simply add the apostrophe after the *s*:

the girls' dresses

the shops' windows

If the noun becomes an irregular plural, we add the apostrophe to the end of the plural noun and the *s* follows on:

the people's princess

the children's nanny

These rules are, for English, quite straightforward and unchanging, yet everywhere we go we see them misapplied.

If we are talking about one or more nouns possessing something jointly, we only use the apostrophe on the last one. For example:

Jack, Jill and Mary's aunt

Lewisham, Islington and Lambeth's hospital trusts

It is also important to remember that when we replace the noun with a pronoun, we do not use an apostrophe.

The book was *hers.*
The people waved *their* banners.

The only exception to this is the use of *one*, which is now rare. *One* is treated as an ordinary noun in this way: 'One is expected to do *one's* duty.'

One is expected to do one's duty.

Contractions

This is the second main use of the apostrophe. When we have omitted a letter, we replace it with an apostrophe to indicate that it is missing. Here are some examples: *can't, didn't, don't, he's, I've, mustn't, shouldn't, they're, won't, you've …*

As you can see, it is usually the words *are*, *have*, *is* and *not* that lose some letters and contract into one single unit. In formal written text, such as a business letter, it is preferable to use the complete expression, *do not*, *have not*, etc., rather than the contraction.

A Three-Part Problem

So far we have seen where the apostrophe should go. Now we should take a minute to see where it has no place at all. One of the most common errors made with the apostrophe is with the simple, but apparently mystifying, difference between ***its*** and ***it's***. If you understand that *it's* is a **contracted** version of *it is*, and write *it's* only under these circumstances and no other, you will never make the mistake again. Hoorah!

Its, without the apostrophe, *always* refers to something belonging to an animal or object: 'The horse shook its head'; 'The tree has lost its leaves,' and so on.

The final rule about the apostrophe – and this should also be remembered at all costs – is that it is never, under any circumstances, used to make a plural. Their are many, various ways of turning a singular into a plural, as we have seen in the chapter on nouns, but using an apostrophe is not one of them. Ever. Isn't it nice to have at least one, unbreakable rule?

Speech Marks and 'Inverted Commas'

Speech

These raised marks originate from a sign known as the *diple*, which at one time was a printer's mark on the margin of a manuscript to draw attention to part of the text, such as a biblical quotation. Over the years, they were placed within the text and came to indicate speech. In the US, the prevailing tendency is to use double quotation marks, thus: "…", while in the UK the single mark '…' is favoured.

Direct speech is always written within quotation marks. If, within that direct speech we are quoting someone else, we use the opposite style of quotation marks around their words to those we are using for direct speech. That is to say, if we are using *double* quotation marks as a matter of course, we put internal quotations within *single* marks and vice versa.

UK usage: 'I heard a voice call to me. "Mary, look out," it said.'

US usage: "My father told me his life story. 'Son, I want you to remember me', he began."

The tendency in the UK is to place punctuation marks within quotation marks, while in the US, punctuation is placed outside as a matter of course. While the US solution makes life simpler, the UK rule seems more logical: if the punctuation is part of the direct speech, put it within the quotation marks. If the punctuation relates to the rest of the sentence rather than the quoted material, place it on the outside.

Indirect speech requires no quotation marks: He asked his friend if he had said look out.

Essays, Poems, Chapters

Whereas the names of long works of fiction, non-fiction, music, film and so on are usually printed in italics, shorter works tend to appear within quotation marks. These include essays, poems (except very long ones), short stories and songs.

Other Uses

Inverted commas are often used to draw attention to a special word or phrase within a sentence. For example:

The mathematics teacher said that the kind of maps we were studying are called 'topological'.

Mum's 'tempting tuna tartine' was a huge success!

This form can backfire: advertisers – on billboards, in newspapers, on signs – are placing inverted commas around words that they want to highlight. Not a sin in itself, admittedly. Inverted commas do indeed bring attention to certain words, but they do not always do it in a good way. The writers of these signs seem not to realize that inverted commas around a word can have the opposite effect from the one intended: they make the reader sceptical.

If we are told that milk is 'organic' and from 'local' farms, we interpret this (or we should) as meaning that the producer has *called* the milk organic, but that it might contain more antibiotics than a hospital dispensary. The inverted commas around the word 'local' imply that the farm may be local if you are living on the Isle of Skye, but actually gallons of diesel are used in transporting the milk to you.

On seeing these inverted commas, the reader mentally puts the phrase 'so-called' in front of every word decorated with them. They scream *fake* and should be completely avoided – unless your intention is to be ironic.

'Loser' Lennie wins Lottery.

Politician's 'expenses' exposed.

In each of these, the writer is saying that the words in inverted commas are used either euphemistically or deliberately to deceive. Take them with a pinch of salt.

Brackets: Separate Measures

Round brackets (officially known as *parentheses*) are most commonly used to cordon off a separate thought within a sentence. If the brackets are correctly placed, the sentence will read perfectly well without the bracketed material, but it will lack a bit of spice. The idea expressed within brackets should be little more than a brief diversion; a thought that has occurred to the writer while they are explaining something else. It should never take over the main thrust of the sentence.

Supplementary material may also be given within parentheses, so they may be used for examples and details such as dates:

Add the dry ingredients (sugar, flour, baking powder) to the eggs.

Or

Napoleon's invasion of Russia (1812) resulted in calamity.

These samples always take round brackets (). If, however, we need to insert additional information within brackets, we use square brackets []. These may also be used to place an editorial comment within a text: 'Father Christmas has a hoary [*sic*] beard.' In this example, the editor is saying 'I know this might look odd and you might think I mean "hairy", but actually it is correct.' (By the way, *sic* is from the Latin and means 'thus' or 'so it is'.)

You do not put a comma before an opening bracket, only after a closing bracket – unless the brackets contain a complete sentence – in which case the full stop ending that sentence goes inside the closing bracket.

Sometimes a pair of dashes may be used to separate secondary information from the main idea of a sentence. A dash is less formal and tends to follow the rhythms of speech more than the bracket. Your choice will depend on the context of your writing and the effect you wish to achieve.

Hyphens: Join and Divide

The hyphen is a dual-purpose punctuation mark; it puts words together and it keeps them apart. It is a small dash on the keyboard, and is almost never surrounded by blank space (the exception being in such cases such as *man- and womankind*, where it implies that something is missing; in this case the suffix *kind* which would otherwise be appended to 'man') but takes the place of a space when you are writing or typing.

When an adjective is composed of two words and precedes the noun which it describes, the two words should be hyphenated. There is the world of difference between *a little worn dress* (small and worn-out) and *a little-worn dress* (nearly new). The hyphen is not required if it does not precede the noun as its meaning is clear. Examples of the hyphen being used in this way include:

That is an eye-catching outfit.

That outfit is eye catching. (However, 'eye-catching' being an accepted expression, it could just as well retain its hyphen here.)

Phrases that act as an adjective should also take hyphens to show that they act together to describe the object:

A round-the-world trip

A once-in-a-lifetime occasion

An off-the-peg suit

Here is Evelyn Waugh demonstrating his skill with hyphenated adjectives:

> She was a middle-aged, well-preserved, well-dressed, well-mannered woman such as I had seen in countless public places.
>
> —Evelyn Waugh, *Brideshead Revisited*

The hyphens and commas allow the adjectives to build into a compact, detailed description that gives the reader a great deal of information in a very concise manner. In fact Waugh manages to sum up this woman, her appearance, her age, her background and her demeanour with admirable clarity and brevity.

Phrases such as *well-informed*, *ill-mannered* and *self-motivated* also take hyphens as they clarify the way in which the adjective has been formed and make for easier reading.

Another use of the hyphen is to join a prefix to a proper noun, such as *anti-American feeling* or *post-Georgian architecture*.

Certain words take a hyphen to distinguish their meaning from those that do not. *A re-formed rock band*, for example, is a very different entity from *a reformed rock band*. Where the hyphen is used, the meaning of the prefix comes into play – *re* meaning again – but where there is no hyphen, we are using a different verb that happens to begin with the letters *re*. Relay, for example, means to impart some information, but re-lay might mean putting down a new carpet on the floor.

Numbers from 21 to 99, and so on, take hyphens when written out (*thirty-four*, *one hundred and thirty-four*, etc.), as do fractions when written in words (*seven-eighths*).

It has recently become more common to join together compound nouns without using a hyphen: *fencepost*, *bookshelf*, *chimneypot*, and so on.

But where the two nouns form a compound that is bulky and inelegant, the two are separated by a hyphen:

Flower-bud, lamp-post, film-maker

As these are so variable, it is probably best to check them in a dictionary before committing them to paper.

Hyphens are no longer required in adverbial phrases such as *widely held belief* or *slowly moving vehicle*, but they are still commonly found here and there are a great many worse sins you can commit than this one.

The Dash: Drawing the Line

O ne of the main uses of the dash (or 'en rule') is very similar to that of the bracket: to separate a subordinate idea from the main substance of a sentence.

Dashes break up a sentence in an informal way, allowing two related ideas to be held together, but loosely. For example:

I watched that film you lent me – what a tearjerker!

While it would not be wrong to use a semicolon in these examples, the dash gives the impression of excitement and emotion behind the words.

In a similar way, dashes can be used to attach an afterthought to a sentence, again following speech patterns:

Please bring back a bottle of wine when you come to dinner – red would be best.

It's snowing – don't forget your gloves.

Dashes, like commas, may be used to balance a sentence:

His face was white, fanatical, and rather beautiful – the expression that all English faces were to wear at Chandrapore for many days.

—E. M. Forster, *A Passage to India*

Here commas are replaced by dashes in examples taken from the section on commas:

'One day – when the snow has melted – we should visit your mother.'

'You'll be home for dinner tonight – won't you?'

'Some people enjoy champagne – others prosecco.'

It is noticeable that dashes as well as giving more balance, can lend a greater weight to the statements: when the snow has melted, definitely not now; not sure you'll be home for supper, but hope so.

They often appear in older texts when a sentence or word is left incomplete, as a longer dash (or 'em rule'): 'We shall go no further with the —th than the city gates' and 'Mrs S—, Miss Emmy, and Mr Joseph in India' – both from *Vanity Fair*, by William Makepeace Thackeray.

In these examples, the dash is used to indicate the author's discretion. He is not prepared to divulge the number of the regiment or the lady in question and we must guess what and to whom he is referring. Today, the writer is more likely either to use a real name or to invent something.

Sometimes the dash is used to indicate the word *to* in a range of numbers, letters, dates etc. For example:

The A–Z map

The 1914–1918 War

While the dash has a great many uses, it does break up a text and interrupts its flow. For this reason, it should be used with precision to avoid jerkiness and confusion.

Spelling It Out

The English language does not make life easy for those of us who wish to spell correctly; in fact, it is one of the least phonetic languages in the world. The sounds we write do not have a consistent and reliable connection to the sounds we make when we read them and vice versa. If I had written my first sentence phonetically, it would look like this:

> The Inglish langwidge duz not make life eazy for thoze of us hoo wish to spell correctly; in fact, it is wun of the leest fonetic langwidges in the werld.

As you can see, very few of the words are spelled as they sound (or pronounced as they are spelled, as we shall see in the next chapter). Some are almost unrecognizable. Much of this difficulty results from the way the language has developed over the centuries, with words being absorbed from the languages of successive invaders. It has also continued to adopt new words from other languages to this day – including words from countries the British in turn colonized: from Urdu and Hindi we have such household words as *bungalow*, *pyjamas*, *shampoo* and *shawl*, as well as *thug*; from West Africa we have, for example, *banana*, *cola* and *zombie*; from Chinese, *gung-ho*, *tea*, *tycoon*; from Malay, *caddy*, *ketchup*, *gingham*.

Does it matter if we misspell words? In a word – yes. However confusing the spelling might be, if everybody spelled words as they heard them, it would be even more confusing.

Good spelling demonstrates attention to detail. A job application that contains wrongly spelled words and poor punctuation reflects badly on the writer. If you do not take the trouble to check your work and you misspell words in an application or CV, it suggests you might not take enough trouble with the job you are applying for, or, indeed that you don't care whether or not you get the appointment (for tips on wording a job application see pp. 156–8). In fact, some employers have a 'three strikes and you're out' rule – more than three errors in your application and they will not give it any further consideration.

It is important to remember that your computer's word-processing program's spelling checker will not do the job for you. It only draws your attention to a word that is spelled incorrectly and it may leave you with the correct spelling of the wrong word. It cannot guess what you are trying to type, and it is not without the odd mistake. Check spellings in a dictionary if you are in doubt; that way you know you have spelled the right word correctly. In this manner, you can be sure of writing what you mean.

Illogical and changeable as English spelling may be, it

is nevertheless the third most widely spoken language in the world (after Mandarin and Spanish). It reigns supreme in scientific, business and international exchanges of any kind, and is said to be the internationally preferred second language.

Some Basic Spelling Rules

- A *q* is nearly always followed by a *u* – *quiet, quiz, quota,* etc.
- A word that ends with a *v* sound is always spelled with a *ve* – *votive, motive, love, have,* etc.
- There is no *uv* in English, not even *luv*; we always use an *o*, though the sound is 'uh' – *cover, dove, move,* etc.

- There are seven words in English that begin with the sound 'all', but are only spelled with one *l* – *altogether*, *always*, *alternative*, *altar*, *already*, *alternate*, *alter*.

- Words to which a prefix has been added do not change their spelling. For example *unhappy*, *misspell*, *antibiotic*, etc.

- Words that end with the sound *full* always take only one *l* – *hopeful*, *spoonful*, *wishful*, etc.

- When words that end in *-al*, *-il* or *-ul*, are made into adverbs, they take a double *l* – *gradual/gradually*, *magical/magically*, *hopeful/hopefully*, *beautiful/beautifully*, and so on.

- The *i* before *e* rule is limited. Originally, it stated that *i* goes before *e* except after *c*, but this does not fit very often as we have words like *deity*, *neighbour*, *neither* or *weight*. The rule was modified so that if the sound made was an *ee*, *i* should go before *e* except after *c*. But there are still rule-breakers – take *caffeine* or *weird* – and the rule hardly applies. If in doubt, check in a dictionary.

- With words like *licence/license* and *practice/practise*, remember that the *c* is used if the word is a noun. If you are using the word as a verb, the *s* form should be used. (A little memory aid – think of the words *advise* and *advice*: these are pronounced differently from each other so we know which is which – and therefore that the verb is the one with an *s*.)

A Note About –Ise and –Ize

The sharper-eyed of you will have noticed that sometimes a word is spelled with -ise *and sometimes with* -ize, *and may well have wondered why. In British English, there are three differently spelled verb endings that are pronounced 'eyes'. They are* -yse, -ise *and* -ize, *and the difference in spelling is because they come from different root words. The* -yse *endings, like* paralyse, analyse *have nouns ending in* -is, *as in* analysis. *They are easy to spot and should not have a* z *except in US English.*

The verbs of the second group always take -ise *in UK English – they include* advertise, exercise, improvise, televise.

The majority of the 'eyes' verbs fall in the third group and can have either -ise *or* -ize *as an ending – in the US* -ize *is always used, in the UK both are used but* -ise *predominates.*

You can use either, but do check in a dictionary if you are uncertain – and do not mix up -ize *and* -ise *spellings in a single piece of writing.*

- *-able* and *-ible*: comparatively few words take the *-ible* ending, which is from the Latin ending *-ibilis* (*audible, compatible, horrible, visible*); the *-able* is also often Latin in origin (from the ending *-abilis*). There are many *-able* words, and they are continually being added to (*fossilizable, networkable* are recent additions to the *Oxford English Dictionary*) and the suffix may be added to virtually any verb where necessary (*emailable*, for instance); more established *-able* words include *drinkable, enjoyable, washable*, etc. The rule, in theory, is that if you remove *-able* from a word, you should be left with a complete word; remove *-ible* and you are left with an incomplete word. But there are, of course, exceptions: *affable, friable, immutable, accessible, flexible, suggestible...*

The Homonym Family

Even the briefest look at any dictionary will verify that for a high percentage of the words listed, there is more than one meaning. Words that are spelled the same but have different meanings are known as **homonyms** when they are pronounced the same, and **homographs** when they are pronounced differently. If they are pronounced the same but are spelled differently, as well as having different meanings, they are **homophones**. (In case you were wondering – the prefix is from the Greek *homos*, meaning 'same'.)

Homonyms

(NB Many of these have more than the two different meanings shown)

Bark: *sound made by dogs /a tree's 'skin'*

Fair: *just, even-handed/fête, social event or exhibition*

Hide: *to conceal/the skin of an animal*

Jam: *fruit preserve/to wedge or push in forcibly*

Lap: *to lick up/circuit of a racetrack*

Lie: *an untruth, or to tell one/to be in a more or less horizontal position*

Loom: *to appear in vague and possibly menacing form/a contraption for weaving on*

Mail: *to send by post, letters and parcels/flexible metal armour*

Page: *to call over public address system/youth employed by hotels, etc.*

Pole: *northern or southern end of Earth's axis/a long straight rod of wood or metal*

Pound: *to thump repeatedly/a unit of weight*

Stalk: *to follow stealthily/main stem of plant*

Homophones

Homophones are loved by comedians because they lead to puns. We expect one meaning of a word and are presented with another. Result: confusion, hilarity. The best puns are extremely witty; many, however, rely on timing and lose much in repetition. A famous example is the *Two Ronnies* sketch in which fork handles are confused with four candles (type it into an Internet search engine to watch the whole thing).

Try these jokes, which rely on homophones and work only when read aloud:

Venison's dear, isn't it?

And

Q: What's your favourite wine?
A: You don't buy me flowers any more.

As you can see, the confusion of *deer* and *dear* is the crux of the first joke, while the confusion between *wine* and *whine* is at the heart of the second. In his book *Spellbound*, James Essinger mentions seeing a sign in a public building that read 'Closed due to leeks'. How did these vegetables cause such damage? One of the more irritating stickers seen on the back of cars reads 'If you can read this your too close'. My too close? What is a 'too close'? I'm sure I don't have one, whatever it is.

A Selection of Homophones

The following sound the same but differ in spelling and meaning:

air – oxygen, nitrogen, etc.   *heir* – one who inherits
e'er – poetic ever   *ere* – poetic before

bored – experiencing tedium   *board* – plank of wood

cereal – grain   *serial* – in instalments

chews – eats   *choose* – select

fate – destiny   *fête* – celebrate

flaw – imperfection   *floor* – ground

gamble – bet   *gambol* – frolic

groan – moan   *grown* – got bigger

hear – make out sounds   *here* – in this place

loan – something borrowed   *lone* – solitary

male – masculine   *mail* – post

prise — lever open
prize — reward

pries — acts intrusively

sail — travel by boat

sale — process of selling

sense — awareness, feeling
cents — US currency

scents — smells

wait — allow time to pass

weight — heaviness

Homographs

These can really confuse the incautious reader. The words are spelled the same, but their meanings are different. Your only clue to their meanings is the context in which they are used. So pay attention to what you are reading!

Silly Sentences to Illustrate Homographs

*The **august** professor is coming to give a talk in **August**.* (Stress on *gust* in first, on *au* in second.)

*The violinist gave a **bow** and dropped his **bow**.* (First rhymes with *cow*, second with *no*.)

*I don't want him to **desert** me in the **desert**.* (First has stress on second syllable; second has stress on first syllable.)

*As she made her **entrance**, she presented a sight to **entrance** even the most cynical.* (Stress on *en* in first, *ance* in second.)

*Even though he was an **invalid** they would not let him through because his papers were **invalid**.* (Stress on *in* in first and *val* in second.)

*The **lead** singer's comments went down like a **lead** balloon.* (First rhymes with *feed*, second with *red*.)

*She **lives** to hear about celebrities' **lives**.* (First rhymes with *gives*, second with *hives*.)

*The **minute** hand on this watch is **minute**; I can hardly see it.* (First has stress on short *in*, second has long *i*: 'my newt'.)

*Have you **read** that article yet? Oh, you must **read** it.* (First sounds like *red*, second rhymes with *seed*.)

*They had a **row** as to who was to **row** the boat.* (First rhymes with *cow*, second with *so*.)

*She was in **tears** about the **tears** across her dress.* (First rhymes with *ears*, second rhymes with *airs*.)

*She **wound** the bandage round the **wound**.* (First rhymes with *round*, second rhymes with *mooned*.)

Tips for Accurate Spelling

Here are a few user-friendly mnemonics (memory aids) to help you learn and retain some of the trickier words that English has to offer. These – often rather silly – phrases are much more memorable than a string of letters.

Accommodate: A Cosy Cottage Of Mellow Maple Or Dark Ash To Enter

Business: Bears Use Sugar In Nescafé, Elephants Spill Sugar

Diarrhoea: Died In A Rolls Royce Having Over-Eaten Again

Necessary: Never Eat Cake, Eat Salmon Sandwiches And Remain Young

Professor: Pigs Roam Over Fields Eating Sausage Sandwiches Or Rolls

If you know that there are certain words that always cause you problems, you can make up your own memory-jogger. Here are some other tips for remembering those tricky words that look wrong no matter how you spell them.

Separate – find a rat: sep-**a-rat**-e.

Lose, loose – a noose can be loose; it can never be lose. Lose means mislaid. (Perhaps it has lost an 'o'.) Note that the *s* in 'lose' has a *z* sound, but not in 'loose'.

Rhyme and rhythm – both start with *rhy*. You can remember the ending of rhythm because it makes your Two Hips Move.

Onomatopoeia – this is a really tricky one with all the vowels crowded together. However, if you think of the phrase Show Me My Way, you have the appropriate sounds (O, E, I, A) and can place the letters in the correct order accordingly.

Stationary and stationery – stationery with an *e* is for paper and Envelopes. Stationary with an *a* is a train (which contains an *a*) stopped at a station.

More Silent Letters to Remember

B – *doubt, comb, numb, thumb*

D – *adjust, edge, handsome, Wednesday*

G – *campaign, design, gnarled, gnome, resign, through*

H – *rhyme, rhythm, whether, white*

K – *knife, knight, knock, know*

L – *calf, colonel, embalm, walk, yolk*

N – *column, damn, solemn*

P – *pneumonia, psychology, receipt*

T – *castle, listen, soften*

U – *biscuit, building, guard, tongue*

W – *sword, two, wrist, wrong*

Cian, sion and tion

The endings *-cian*, *-sion* and *-tion* make the sounds 'shun' or 'zhun', and usually turn verbs into nouns.

- If the root word ends in *d* the new ending is nearly always *-sion* – but we have *retard/retardation*.

- If the root word ends in an *s* the new ending will be *-sion*: *compress/compression*.

- If the root word ends in a *t* sound, the noun from it

will end in *-tion*, as in *complete/completion*, or in *-sion* as in *permit/permission*.

- If the *-shun* ending is in a word describing a person, the ending will be spelled *-cian*, as in *musician*, *optician*, *politician*, *technician*, etc.

- If the sound of the last syllable is a heavy *zhun* sound, the ending will be *-sion*: *vision*, *confusion*, etc.

- How many exceptions to these rules can you find?

Avoiding Pitfalls . . .

1. When tackling a long word, divide it up into syllables and pay extra attention to double letters.

2. When writing compound words, that is a word comprised of two that have been pushed together to make one word, imagine splitting it back into two words to ensure that you do not omit any letters, e.g. *lampshade*, *roommate*, *tabletop*, etc.

3. Beware of silent letters. English has many of these, as we have seen when discussing pronunciation. (Remember, too, that there are plenty of exceptions.)

4. Poor spelling is often interpreted as carelessness in the writer – it is always worth a last spelling check on any piece of writing.

5. There is a list of frequently misspelled words on p. 177.

Perfect Pronunciation

In most European languages, pronunciation presents far fewer problems than it does in English. For the English speaker, the problems with pronouncing European words tend to revolve around actually making the right sounds – gutturals and rolled *r*s in particular. But as to how the word should sound – there are rules, and as long as we follow these rules, we should be all right …

The English language, however, can play some very unkind tricks on the unwary. It is tempting, having learned a new word, to think we can use the same sounds for similar-looking words. Not so. Their pronunciation can actually be quite different:

bough/cough/enough/
    through
comb/tomb
gorse/worse

love/move
speak/steak
sieve/grieve
wind/kind

Much of the problem can be explained by the history of individual words. Many silent letters are a result of our multi-layered language. We have seen how waves of invaders introduced new words into the English language, to the extent that when the Roman alphabet was introduced it became necessary to combine certain letters in order to create new sounds. The most common of these is *th*, originally represented by the Old English eth and thorn.

A revival of interest in Latin and ancient Greek in the sixteenth century complicated things even further. Believing that it would be helpful if we knew that words like debt came from the Latin *debitum*, linguists put the *b* back into *dette* thus creating a range of silent letters to confuse things still further. A number of words of Greek origin have a silent *p – psychology, pneumonia, pterosaur –* or *ph* for the *f* sound

A pterosaur has a silent pee.

as in *sophisticated*. (The *p* was added to *ptarmigan* in the mistaken belief that the word was Greek; it in fact derives from Scottish Gaelic *tármachan*.)

How the Letters are Pronounced: A Short Guide

First the **vowel** sounds. These are the sounds we make with an open mouth so that air can pass over the vocal cords, causing them to vibrate. They are usually found between consonants, sandwiched in the middle, allowing us to open the mouth between consonants. Their pronunciation can vary for a number of reasons, in general in accordance with the other letters in the word as it is written. Generally speaking, the vowels – *a*, *e*, *i*, *o*, *u* and *y* – have at least one long and one short sound, and variations on these.

Aa short as in *mat*, or *another*; long as in *cake*, or *part or paw*

Ee short as in *bet*; or *the*; long as in *she*

Ii short as in *pin*; long as in *time*

Oo short as in *pot*; long as in *root*

Uu short as in *hut* or *put*; long as in *tune*

Yy stands in for *i* – short as in *pretty*; long as in *my*

This is vastly simplified – vowel and consonant sounds vary, sometimes hugely, sometimes very slightly. In the written word, these variations may be indicated (but not always, and not consistently) by the letters that might follow them. This can, as we shall see, be a help in spelling a word. Or it can cause further confusion, especially when a quite unexpected letter is used to give a sound – for instance the *u* in *busy* is pronounced as a short *i*.

While, to paraphrase the *Oxford English Dictionary*, vowels consist of pure voice or musical sound, **consonants** are simple noises wholly or mainly produced in the mouth, or the mouth and nose. They make up the larger part of the alphabet, some of the letters being 'hard' or 'soft', or some being combined to make certain sounds. On the whole, there are fewer variations in sound among individual consonants. The most common are included in the list of consonants below.

Bb   sounds as you would expect, but is occasionally silent, as at the end of *bomb*

Cc   can be hard as in *cat*, or soft as in *certain*; combines with *h* to make *ch* as in *chase*, occasionally with a softer sound as in *machine* (NB some *ch* combinations give a hard *see*, as in *chasm* or *ache*)

Dd   sounds as you would expect, very occasionally silent as in *adjust, handkerchief*

Ff   has an *f* sound as in *off*, and *v* sound as in *of*

Gg   can be hard as in *go*, soft as in *gentle,* or combine with *n* to make nasal *ng*, as in *long*

Hh   can be voiced ('aspirated') as in *have*, or silent as in *hour*, and it changes the sounds made by the consonants *c, s* and *t*

Jj   sounds as you would expect, very occasionally given a softer sound as in *abjure*

Kk, Ll, Mm   all sound as you would suppose, except that *l* is occasionally silent, as in *balmy*, and *k* is sometimes silent, as in *knee*

Nn   can be combined with *g* to make a nasal sound as in *hanging*, and is sometimes silent, as in *autumn*

Pp   can be combined with *h* to make an *f* sound as in *philosophy*; is occasionally silent as in *pneumatic*

Qq   is combined with *u* and makes a *kw* sound as in *queen*, or sometimes a plain *k* sound as in *quoit*, *queue*, or as in the suffix *–esque*; appears without the *u* in words of foreign origin as in the Gulf state of *Qatar* or the Chinese *qigong* (similar to tai chi)

Rr   lengthens vowels as in *pat* and *part*

Ss   has an *s* sound as in *snake*, and sometimes a *z* sound as in *cosy* (which, incidentally, is spelled *cozy* in the US); it can be combined with *h* to make *sh* as in ***sharp***; and occasionally with *ch* to make a *sh* sound as (British) *schedule* or a *sk* sound as in *school*

Tt   combines with *h* to make *th* as in ***think***, or as in ***this***

Vv   sounds as you would expect

Ww when it follows vowels it can alter their sound, as in *raw* or *stew*; occasionally silent, as in *who* or *wrap*

Xx   sounds as you would expect

Yy   can also be a vowel

Zz   is perhaps appropriately used to denote having fallen asleep ...

We make many other sounds, which are represented (not always that logically) by consonants, or combinations – as in *measure*, where the *s* is a soft *z*; or *attention*, where the *ti* is *sh*. These, like the ones listed above, are all well known to us and generally present no problems to fluent English speakers.

Hints on Pronunciation for Foreigners

I take it you already know
Of **tough** *and* **bough** *and* **cough** *and* **dough**?
Others may stumble, but not you,
On **hiccough, thorough, lough** *and* **through**?
Well done! And now you wish, perhaps,
To learn of less familiar traps?
Beware of **heard**, *a dreadful word*
That looks like **beard** *and sounds like* **bird**,
And **dead**: *it's said like* **bed**, *not* **bead** –
*For goodness' sake don't call it '***deed***'!*
Watch out for **meat** *and* **great** *and* **threat**
(They rhyme with **suite** *and* **straight** *and* **debt***).*
A **moth** *is not a moth in* **mother**,
Nor **both** *in* **bother**, **broth** *in* **brother**,

> *And* **here** *is not a match for* **there**
> *Nor* **dear** *and* **fear** *for* **bear** *and* **pear;**
> *And then there's* **dose** *and* **rose** *and* **lose** –
> *Just look them up –* *and* **goose** *and* **choose,**
> *And* **cork** *and* **work** *and* **card** *and* **ward,**
> *And* **font** *and* **front** *and* **word** *and* **sword,**
> *And* **do** *and* **go** *and* **thwart** *and* **cart** –
> *Come, come, I've hardly made a start!*
> *A dreadful language? Man alive!*
> *I'd mastered it when I was five!*
> —Anonymous

Ssh! Silent Letters

Written English is strewn with silent letters, making both spelling and pronunciation something of a minefield. There are some things to look out for that will help – a word beginning with *ps* or *kn*, for example, when spoken will not actually contain these sounds and one of the letters will be silent. As a rule (but remember, in the English language, rules always have exceptions), if it is difficult to vocalize each consonant when they are combined, the likelihood is that one of them is silent. Here are some more patterns to help us:

G is not usually pronounced when followed by an *n*, as in *feign*, *gnome*, *reign*, *sign* – there are exceptions, such as *recognize* or *signature*.

GH is not pronounced before a *t* or at the end of many words: *daughter* (but in the similarly constructed *laughter*, *gh* is pronounced *f*), *right*, *through*, *weigh*

H is not usually pronounced following *w*: *whale*, *what*, *wheel*, *why* (it is sometimes voiced at the start, however, especially for dramatic effect: 'And *HWAT* are you doing?', and indeed the Old English word was *hwæt*)

K at the beginning of a word is not pronounced when followed by an *n*: *knack*, *knee*, *knife*, *knowledge*

L is not usually pronounced before *d*, *f* or *m* if they come at the end the word: *calm*; *half* (but *halfpenny* is traditionally pronounced 'ha'penny', and the *l* is pronounced in *self*); *salmon* (but pronounced in *salmonella*); *should* (but pronounced in *bold*, *mould*, *scald*)

N is not pronounced after an *m* at the end of a word: *autumn* (pronounced in *autumnal*); *hymn* (pronounced in *hymnal*)

P is not pronounced at the beginning of words often deriving from Greek: *pneumonia*, *psalm*, *psittacosis*, *psychiatry*, *ptarmigan* (the last, as mentioned earlier, being owed to a classicist who assumed the word was of Greek derivation whereas it is from the Scottish Gaelic)

W is not pronounced at the beginning of a word when followed by an *r*, as in *wrath*, *write*, *wrestle* (silent *t* here too), and *wrong*, or sometimes when followed by *ho*: *who*, *whole*, *whom*, *whose*

Other Pronunciation Oddities

Soft and Hard C and G

The rule: the letter *c* is hard (with a *k* sound) when followed by *a*, *o*, *u* or most consonants – for example, *coat*, *climb*, *acorn*, *increase*, *uncle*. (There always has to be at least one exception: *caesarean* is pronounced with a soft *c*.)

And the *c* is soft (with an *s* sound) when followed by *e*, *i* or *y*, as in *celebrate*, *citizen*, *pincer* or *cylinder*.

The exceptions: *ceilidh* (pronounced 'kaylee') comes from the Celtic and should be pronounced with a hard *c*; so, properly, should Celt and Celtic – however, the traditional soft *c* sound is also acceptable, and Celtic Football Club retains the soft *c*. Another exception is *arcing*, which is pronounced with a hard *c*, to some people's disappointment. And in *cello* it is pronounced with the *ch* sound of the Italian original.

The letter *g* follows the same rules – to a lesser extent. It is hard (*gh*) when followed by *a*, *o*, *u* and most consonants, as in *ago*, *galaxy*, *glaze*, *golf* or *gull*. In some words, a *u* has been inserted to convert a soft *g* to a hard *g*, as in **guess**, **guide**, **guitar**.

An exception is the word *margarine*, which is today usually pronounced with a soft *g*, and in words like *acknowledgment* when spelled without the *e*, as preferred in the US.

The *g* is soft (with a *j* sound) when followed by e, i and y, as in **agitate**, **general**, **enrage**, **giant**, **gymnasium**, **misogyny**.

There are many exceptions, among them **gear**, **get**, **girl**, **girth** and **gynaecology**.

Off and Of

The pronunciation of these two commonly used words can create confusion for the non-native speaker. Off, meaning at a distance, away from, the opposite of on, etc., is pronounced with the simple f sounds as in fluff, whiff, *or even* phase. *The word* of, *meaning part of or belonging to, is pronounced with a v sound – ov.*

Although the two do not sound exactly alike, writing one for the other is quite common in hurried or careless pieces of writing (and is not picked up by word processors' spelling checkers).

The Ghastlies

Pronouncing words that end in or contain *-augh*, *-aigh*, *-eigh*, *-igh* and *-ough* can be a challenge for the native English speaker – especially the *-ough* words – so how much more difficult it must be for the foreigner trying to learn English. The first thing to remember is that most of the time the *gh* combination is not pronounced at all … but there are – of course – exceptions.

The easy ones to start with: those that end in *-ight*. Quite simply, the *gh* lengthens the *i* so that words like *light* and *tight* rhyme with *bite*.

If the word ends in *-aight*, however, it rhymes with *fate*, as in *straight*.

And if it ends in *-eight*, it might rhyme with *light* and *bite*, as do *height* and *sleight* …

Or it might rhyme with *straight* and *fate*, as do *eight* and *weight*.

Words with *-augh* are not too bad. Most of them rhyme with *sort* – examples include *caught*, *daughter*, *taught*.

But then there are *laugh*, pronounced 'larf', and *draught*, which is pronounced 'draft'. Isn't that daught?

Worse is to come …

although is pronounced to rhyme with *all go*

bough, *plough* rhyme with *brow*, *cow*, etc.

bought, *brought*, *ought*, *thought*, *wrought* all rhyme with *port*, *short*, etc.

borough, *thorough*, *thoroughbred*, etc. – roughly pronounced 'urr-'h' (the *-ough* is what is called a **schwa**, see p.145)

cough, *trough* (*gh* combination has '*ff*' sound) rhyme with *off*

dough, *though* rhyme with *foe*, *slow*, etc.

drought rhymes with *out*, *spout*, etc.

hiccough (*gh* combination has '*p*' sound) rhymes with *pick-up* and is usually more sensibly spelled 'hiccup'

hough (rare) pronounced 'hock', which is what it means (a leg joint)

lough (body of water) is pronounced like the Scots *loch* ('lokh')

rough, *tough* ('*ff*' again) are pronounced to rhyme with *fluff*, *stuff*, etc.

slough (swamp, and the town of that name) rhymes with *cow*, *now*, etc.

slough (to shed skin, as snakes do, or slide down as soil or rock might do) rhymes with *cuff*, *fluff*, etc.

through pronounced 'throo' (rhyming with *crew*, *true* etc.)

Reducing the Stress

Unlike French and Spanish, for instance, which are 'syllable-timed' languages (in which each syllable has the same time-duration), English, along with other Germanic languages, is 'stress-timed'. This means that stresses occur at regular intervals, regardless of the number of syllables – so, to keep the stress pattern regular, the important words are stressed, while the relatively unimportant words (typically articles – *a*, *the* – prepositions – *of*,

Elision

When English is spoken quickly elision *occurs. This is when vowels are omitted and sounds run together. In words ending in an 'ary' sound, for example, where the 'a' sound is normally a schwa, with the emphasis on the first syllable, the end becomes 'ry' – the schwa is swallowed up – so that* temporary *is pronounced 'temprary' and* secretary *is 'secretry',* cemetery *becomes 'cemety' and* necessary *becomes 'necessry'. This is considered 'acceptable', but it is often taken one step further, so that temporary becomes 'tempry' and* secretary *becomes 'seketry' and* library *becomes 'libry', which really isn't necessry.*

for, etc. – or conjunctions – *and, or*) are shortened, weakened, hurried over – sometimes contracted so you might hear ''Sraining cats 'n' dogs' or 'he shouldn't've done that'. Or they might be elided (see Elision above.)

The same thing happens within individual words. While stressed syllables maintain the full vowel sound, unstressed syllables are weakened. The most common sound in the English language is that of the unstressed syllable – **schwa** (or **shwa**), the name derived from the Hebrew for 'neutral vowel sound', 'emptiness'. It is usually indicated by /ə/ in the International Phonetic Alphabet.

The schwa is often found – but, as may be seen below, not always – in the middle of a word; and is generally pronounced something like 'uh'. For many people studying English as a foreign language, knowing about the schwa will help them improve their pronunciation and speak with a more English rhythm.

In the following words, the schwa is shown in bold:

*B**a**nana, descend**a**nt, exhil**a**rate, postm**a**n*
*App**a**rent, aqu**e**duct, probl**e**m, synth**e**sis*
*Comp**a**tible, exp**e**riment, penc**i**l, pup**i**l*
*Broth**e**r, gall**o**p, less**o**n, tom**o**rrow*
*B**u**t, cent**u**ry, s**u**pport, medi**u**m*
*Mis**o**gyny, meth**y**lated, syr**i**nge, zeph**y**r*
*D**oe**s, meas**u**re, mount**ai**n, oce**a**n, south**e**rn, theatr**e**,*
 *thor**ough***

Because any vowel can be a schwa, it is often the cause of spelling errors: 'seperate', 'indispensible', 'cemetary', 'desparate' are all common misspellings, and many people find themselves struggling to decide between *dependent* and *dependant*. (Both are correct, but the first is an adjective and the second a noun.)

Another cause of confusion is that the stress can be shifted from one syllable to another to alter a word's meaning while retaining its spelling – usually switching between noun and verb. Thus you may have a **pre**sent (stress on first syllable) or gift that you are going to pres**ent** (stress on second) or give to your friend. Or an athlete may break a world **rec**ord (stress on first) in a 10,000-metre race, but his father forgot to re**cord** (stress on second) the event.

Correspondence Course

Our grasp of English is most tested when it comes to written communication – while anyone can dash off a quick scrawl to a flatmate about missing milk, it becomes imperative to communicate clearly when writing an email or letter to a client, organization or potential employer. If you write a good letter, the chances are that it will be appreciated, and that you will get a comparatively prompt, pleasant and helpful response.

Eloquent Emails

If you are writing to a stranger and you do not know their name, start the email 'Dear Sir' or 'Dear Madam'; otherwise address them as 'Dear Mr/Mrs/Ms/Miss [Name]'. It is acceptable to end emails with a simple 'Kind regards' or 'Best wishes'. Always be polite; keep the message brief and clear; and check spelling and punctuation. If you are sending additional data (a document or a photograph), remember to attach it – and be sure that you are sending the right material.

Emails tend to become less formal faster than letters; a lengthy exchange of emails between two people can become nearly as brief as texts. Emails between friends might begin with 'Dear So-and-so', or 'Hello' or 'Hi', and end just as you would a casual letter.

In all cases, be careful that you have the other person's email address correct – it takes a single click to send an email to the wrong person, which could be unfortunate.

Never put confidential details such as debit card numbers – or anything that could be a security risk – in emails.

Lively Letters

There are degrees of formality in letter writing. Formal letters could be business letters, letters to banks or insurance companies, letters complaining to companies about their goods or services, job-application letters, and so forth. However, there are some general rules to stick to when putting pen to paper (or fingers to keyboard, for that matter) for a posted letter.

1. Always put your address in the top right-hand corner (unless you are using headed paper, in which case it will already be printed across the top).

   You do not put your name there, but you can include your telephone number and email address:

   44 Lettercare Road
   London SW25 4NO
   Tel: 0201234567
   email: norman.bates@batesmotel.com

2. Write the name and address of the person you are writing to on the left-hand side, on the line below the last line of your address. If you do not know the name, at least try to put a job title: Head of Security, Marketing Manager, etc., as shown overleaf.

Ms Amina Khan [or e.g., Personnel Officer]
Moneybags Bank Plc
Miser Street
London EC4 8PR

3. Do not forget the date – this can go to the right or left, beneath the address details. In Britain, the preferred formats are 1 April 2012 or 1st April 2012.

4. Begin the letter with 'Dear Sir or Madam' if you do not know the name, or 'Dear Mr/Mrs/Miss/Ms/Dr' and the surname. If you do not know whether a woman uses 'Miss' or 'Mrs' use 'Ms', which applies to both.

5. If you have a reference (for example, if that person has written to you and has put a reference number at the top of their letter), put it above the main text of your letter. If you are writing to your bank, put your account number, sort code and account name here.

6. Write what you have to say (for ease of reading, use 1.5 spacing in preference to single spacing), keeping it short, to the point and clear.

    Some people like to divide letters into three paragraphs: the first a brief explanation of the letter's purpose: 'I am writing to ask you to increase my over-draft …', or 'Thank you for your letter of 29th March, ref. 0x00x0 …' for example.

The second paragraph will expand on this – why you need the increased overdraft, how long you'll need it for, and so on; or perhaps proceeding to reply to the other person's letter.

And in the third, you might thank the other person for their attention and say what you expect from them, e.g. that an increased overdraft will be possible – and that you look forward to hearing from him/her soon.

7. To end your letter: write on the next line 'Yours sincerely' if you are writing to a named person, or 'Yours faithfully' if you have addressed the letter 'Dear Sir or Madam'.

8. Sign your name with your usual signature (it is very important to sign in pen, even if the rest of the letter is typed), and print your name below. If you think that the other person will not know whether you are male or female (for example, if your name is Hilary or Frances), you can put your preferred title in brackets after it.

9. Check your letter! Mistakes will *not* impress the recipient and will reduce the impact of what you are saying. In a job application, mistakes could lead to your application being rejected out of hand.

   Spelling: the spell checker is useful, but it cannot guess at your meaning; look out especially for homophones, which all too easily creep in: 'I am very accurate – I cannot bare mistakes ...'

   Grammar: check this carefully; read the letter aloud to yourself – maybe ask a friend to look over it too.

   Punctuation: check this carefully as well. Make sure sentences are clear and complete.

   Style: avoid jargon, flowery language and long explanations. In formal letters, avoid colloquialisms (slang), jargon, abbreviations and contractions ('I'm', or 'they've', etc.). Try to be clear and to the point.

   Tone: Always be polite, even in letters of complaint. (Remember that the person who is reading the letter is, in all probability, not the person who committed whatever dastardly crime it is you are complaining about.)

7 Smithfield Drive

Huntingford

Berkshire RG6 10B

Customer Services Manager

Western Trains

Apple Valley Industrial Estates

Swindon SN4 7HQ

17th July 2011

Dear Sir or Madam,

I am writing with reference to a recent train journey I took between Swandon and Huntingford. It was with great disappointment that I noticed that you are no longer stocking Lemon and Poppyseed Shortbread in the buffet car; instead I was forced to purchase two vastly inferior Lemon Thins. I am writing this letter to ask you to reconsider the range and quality of biscuits available on your trains (and to request a free packet of Lemon Thins by way of compensation).

Yours faithfully,

J. Partington

Mr J Partington

Judicious Job Applications

The most important letters most of us write are to prospective employers – written well, they can open doors in your career, even land you the job of your dreams, but badly written, they needlessly narrow your opportunities. Correct layout for your covering letter is imperative – read and study pp. 151–5 – but there are a number of other golden rules that can help you on your way.

Tips for a Convincing Covering letter

Do your homework – make sure you know exactly what qualities they are looking for, as well as researching the company's profile and recent sucesses.

Don't repeat your CV – you should aim to draw the recruiter towards your relevant experince and expand on a couple of key topics that are just briefly mentioned in your CV.

Keep your letter to one page – if you express yourself clearly, this is all the space you should need; any longer and you run the risk of waffle, and losing the attention of your prospective employer.

You, me, we – use the rule of three to explain (1) why you are attracted to this particular company, (2) why your qualities and experience make you an excellent candidate and (3) how parallels between your current work and the work of the company demonstrate that you would fit well into the organization.

CV Dos and Don'ts

DO ensure that your layout is consistent, that headings are the same size, and that spacing between points is equal.

DON'T make it too complicated. Using lots of different type styles and headings only confuses the reader – remember that it is the information that is important, not the eye-catching design (unless, of course, you are going for a job as a designer ...).

DO include clear and simple categories in order of importance. The most common order is Education, Employment, Additional Training and, finally, Interests.

DON'T list spurious hobbies and interests – you could be asked about any aspect of your CV.

DO try to stick to two pages – you have limited time to get yourself across before your potential employer moves on to the next application.

Communicating with Style

Whether we are writing a report for work, a job application, a CV or a letter, the guidelines remain the same: *strive for clarity of thought and expression* and you are well on the way to good prose. This section groups together the common pitfalls, as well as showing the way to writing clear and correct English.

Rhythm, Tone and Other Devices

Listening to the rhythm of our sentences is a crucial element in producing good writing. Sometimes it is necessary to change a word here and there in order to keep the sound 'right' in the reader's head. This is just one weapon in the armoury of a good writer. One of the ways of ensuring that your prose has a good rhythm is to read it aloud when you have written your first draft. Poetry depends greatly on this linguistic tempo for many of its effects, but good prose also requires a good sense of rhythm to 'work'. Other rhetorical effects that can be used to make a piece of writing or a presentation more striking are:

Alliteration – where consonants are repeated, often used in slogans and brand names: Coca-Cola, Dunkin' Donuts, 'Beans Means Heinz'.

Onomatopoeia – using words which sound like the thing, action or state they describe, for example *babble*, *bark*, *murmur*, *fizzle* and *bang*.

Rhyme – subtle rhyme can bring a piece of prose alive, especially when read aloud.

Three-part lists – a tried-and-tested device to form a convincing argument, often used in politics ('Education, education, education' –Tony Blair), but which can also be employed in letters and presentations.

Repetition – though you should avoid tautology at all costs (see p. 172), the deliberate repetition of a central concept can draw together your argument or strengthen your key message.

Imagery – using metaphor and simile (see p. 39) to clever effect gives a visual element to what you are describing that can be very powerful.

Oxymorons – a rhetorical device in which two apparent opposites are put together for effect. Examples are 'a silent scream', 'bittersweet' or 'living dead'. Romeo, in Shakespeare's *Romeo and Juliet*, gets quite carried away with oxymorons: 'O heavy lightness! serious vanity! / Misshapen chaos of well-seeming forms! / Feather of lead, bright smoke, cold fire, sick health! / Still-waking sleep...' (Act 1, Scene 1).

Pitfalls to Avoid

We have covered a great number of rules in this book that, when adhered to diligently, allow us to speak and write correctly. However, there are a number of bad habits that are easy to fall into, but far harder to correct. Some might seem obvious, others less so.

The Double Negative: 'We Don't Need No Education'

We *do* need education, Pink Floyd must be saying in their famous song, 'Another Brick in the Wall' – if we go by the current understanding that two negative words cancel each other out and result in a positive statement.

The stereotypical Cockney thief who says, 'I didn't do nuffin', guv', is guilty of a double negative. Substitute the second negative with the word or prefix 'any', and all becomes clear and correct. The thief should have said, 'I didn't do *any*thing, guv' – or at least, 'I didn't do *any*fink, guv.'

Other examples include: 'I couldn't get no sleep last night', which should be 'I couldn't get *any* sleep last night'; 'I wouldn't go nowhere where it might snow', which should be 'I wouldn't go *any*where where it might snow'; and 'Nobody knows nothing about me', which should be 'Nobody knows *any*thing about me'.

There is a form of double negative that is considered acceptable, where the two negatives combine to convey a weaker positive. This is a rather more subtle use, modifying the positive as it does, and often depends on tone of voice, or on its context, to convey its meaning. It might leave a 'but' in the mind of the reader or listener, it may be ironic, or it damns with faint praise:

It is not that I am not grateful (*but* you should not have done that …)

I do not disagree (*but* do not agree wholeheartedly …)

The difference between these two types of double negative is clear enough. Use the second type with care – remember to get the tone right. Avoid the first unless you are using it jokingly. The most important thing to remember if you are aiming to write clear, unambiguous prose, is not to use double negatives at all.

Me and My Friend

A common mistake made when using pronouns is to confuse the *subject* pronoun with the *object* pronoun. It is well worth taking the time and trouble to get this right, because an error of this kind is very basic and reflects badly on the speaker or writer.

Us girls are going out to a party tonight.

Wrong. That is not to say you're staying in, but perhaps a night curled up with a grammar book would be time well spent. *Us* is the object of the verb and you need the subject in this case: '*We* girls are going out to a party.'

Similar problems occur with *I*, *me* and *my*.

My mum and *me* went shopping.

Wrong. You wouldn't say '*Me* went shopping,' so why say it when you put your mum in the picture? It should be: 'My mum and *I* went shopping.'

Philippa invited John and *I* to her party.

Wrong. No, she didn't – she invited John and *me*.

The trick is quite simple. If you remove other people from the sentence, you can work out far more easily if you should be using *me* or *I*. It is correct to say, 'She handed the books to me,' so it is equally correct to say, 'She handed the books to Simon and me.' If it is correct to say, 'I went by train,' then it is also correct to say, 'He and I went by train.'

And, you and I will have to have a word if you say, 'Between you and I.'

Between you and me
is what it should be.

Conjugation Relations

One very important thing to remember is always, always **match** *the* **verb** *to the* **subject.**

This may be stating the obvious, but it is very common to hear this most basic rule flouted or confused by native English speakers. It is probably only a matter of hours since you heard someone say 'we was' or 'they was', 'he done it', or even 'I were' (but see the Subjunctive, p. 64); you might even have done it yourself. Whereas English can be forgiving of certain errors, this is not one of them. If you conjugate everyday verbs incorrectly, especially in writing, you will be – to put it mildly – doing yourself an injustice. Just ask yourself if Frank Sinatra had been brought up in London, might he have sung 'I done it my way'?

Left Dangling

This seems like a good moment to bring up the subject of **dangling modifiers** (also known as **dangling participles**). As with many grammatical terms, they are not as terrifying as they sound, even though they should be avoided at all times.

'Modifying' really means giving further information about one of the elements of a sentence. To explain the terrifying phenomenon that is the dangling modifier, let me illustrate:

Being a sunny day, we decided to go mushroom-picking.

Wearing gloves at all times, mushrooms can be picked in British woodland throughout the autumn.

If you do not immediately spot the errors in these two sentences, just ask yourself if you could be a sunny day, or when you last saw a mushroom wearing gloves. The writer has given us supplementary information in a subordinate clause, but has wrongly attached it so that it applies to the mushrooms rather than the picker. We should say:

It being/As it was a sunny day, we decided to go mushroom-picking.

Wearing gloves at all times, **you** can pick mushrooms in British woodland throughout the autumn.

If we are modifying a noun, it *must be* the noun that comes next in the sentence.

Q: As a young boy, was your mother very strict with you?

A: Now let's get one thing clear. My mother was never a young boy.

You see: word order is crucial – especially when making jokes! (The correct word order would have been: 'As a young boy, were you treated very strictly by your mother?')

Seven Golden Rules for Good English

The writer George Orwell once compiled a list of six rules for combating clumsy and dull writing (in his essay 'Politics and the English Language') – much of it is as relevant now as it was then, though I have added a final seventh rule of my own.

Rule 1: Never use a metaphor, simile or figure of speech that we are used to seeing in print.

In other words, avoid clichéd or unoriginal writing. Clichés are a little like woodworm: they start eating away at a perfectly good piece of writing and before you know it all the freshness has gone, the structure is damaged beyond repair and the whole thing falls apart.

Clichés

When time is short, as it usually is, we tend to fall back on clichés, as their inventors have already done a lot of the thinking and preparation for us. People know what we mean, they are familiar with the language we are using and, for our part, we do not have to spend time coming up with original ideas. The joy of clichés is that they come fully formed and ready to use; no preparation required. They may be extremely useful if English is your second language as they form building blocks of communication. You will be understood straight away and nobody will hold it against you if you use the odd worn-out phrase.

Here is a list of clichés. Try to avoid them . . . like the plague. (Sorry, clichés have a way of slipping in.)

It's not rocket science

Push the envelope/think outside the box

Can't see the wood for the trees

Over the moon

Sick as a parrot

Skating on thin ice

Walking on eggshells

Get a life

Separate the sheep from the goats/the men from the boys

The bee's knees

In your dreams

You're as old as you feel

I recently heard a woman say that she was going to take two medicines, rather than one, in the hope of curing her problem. 'I'd like to kill two birds with one stone,' she said. It's an odd choice of phrase to begin with, but to be accurate she should have said, 'I'd like to kill one bird with two stones.' This would have shown that she was really thinking about what she was saying and had expressed herself using a lively mixture of the new and the familiar.

Rule 2: Never use a long word when a short one will do.

If a long word is just right for expressing your thoughts, use it. Do not use a long word to make prose seem more complex and difficult or exclusive – or the writer more brilliant – than it really is. There is nothing wrong with long words, but they must be exactly precise in order to clarify your meaning, otherwise they have the opposite effect and block the immediacy of your writing.

Do not 'enquire' rather than 'ask'; 'prevent' rather than 'stop'; or 'attempt' (and certainly not 'endeavour') rather than 'try'. While these are not actually long words, they offend because they are pretentious in the context in which they are used and a simpler word would have done just as well. There is nothing wrong *at all* with small, simple words; they do us great credit when used (not 'utilized') well, and we should not be snobbish or dismissive of them.

Rule 3: If it is possible to cut out a word, cut it out.

We only have to look at some government forms, insurance papers and official documents to see that repetition stands in the way of clarity. While many official papers have to ensure that they have omitted nothing and avoided every loophole, it is obvious that this kind of writing is often irritatingly obscure and hard to fathom. Expressions like 'going forward in time' are pointless and sound like waffle. Just cut them out.

Rule 4: Never use the passive when you can use the active.

In the chapter on sentences, we looked at the difference between the active and the passive voice (p. 65). If we can do it without changing our meaning, we should avoid the passive tense. We end up not knowing who is doing what to whom. Having a clear subject-verb-object structure to our sentence is a great deal less confusing and far more interesting to read.

If you find that your writing relies heavily on the verb *to be* accompanied by past participles (was stolen, is found) followed by the word *by*, you can be fairly sure that you have fallen into the trap of passive writing. Change sentences that follow the pattern 'the postman *was bitten by* the dog' to 'the dog bit the postman' and your writing will immediately pick up speed and gain clarity.

Tautology: Once is Enough

When we unknowingly repeat ourselves, this is known as tautology. *The ruins of an old monastery, for example, are certain to be dilapidated; it goes without saying. We should therefore avoid expressions like 'dilapidated ruins'. If something goes without saying, it is better not to say it.*

Advertisers, however, love tautology. We are offered 'free gifts' and 'added bonuses' all the time. They use tautology for effect. When all their competitors are offering bonuses, they need to step up the interest we have in their product by appearing to offer something more. A bonus on its own is hardly worth considering. But an added bonus: well, that really is something to write home about.

People in business and politicians are often found guilty of tautology. Here are some examples of tautology which are frequently found in soundbites and business announcements: joint cooperation, reiterate again, necessary requirement, totally unanimous, former glories of earlier times ... *You get the point, I'm sure.*

Rule 5: Never use a foreign phrase, scientific word or jargon if you can find an everyday English equivalent.

It is sometimes imperative to use specialist terms when we write, but this depends on whom we are writing for. If we are writing a report for our colleagues, we can be fairly certain that they will understand the professional language that we use. If, however, we are writing for a more general audience, we need to be aware that they will not necessarily be familiar with our specialist terms. One person's myocardial infarction is another person's heart attack. Likewise, the use of foreign phrases can make a piece of writing impenetrable (see box on p. 175).

Readers who do not understand your particular discipline will become irritated if you address them in your own jargon without explaining what the terms actually mean. What, after all, is a *digital product solution*, or an *online offering*? Just because we work in a certain field, we must not assume that the language we use is recognized by everyone. Take a step back from your writing and examine objectively the terms you have used in order to ensure that they are suitable for your readers.

Rule 6: Break any of these rules sooner than say anything barbarous.

Adherence to rules can stifle creativity. If we know and understand the rules fully, we can trust ourselves to break them where necessary. In order to reach that level of under-standing, however, there is one thing that is prescribed: *read, read, read*. You would not attempt to play the violin without listening to music first, would you? Similarly, the only way to get to grips with the language is to immerse yourself fully in all it has to offer. While not everyone has the time to plough through Victorian novels, most people can make the time to read a good feature in a broadsheet paper, or choose a poem each week, just to see what the language can really offer at its best. Why not pick up a short story? Or a book of essays? A novel to read on the way to work?

Rule 7: Write with a love of the language.

This last rule doesn't feature in Orwell's helpful list – but in my mind is every bit as important as the other six. People who have an admiration of the language naturally avoid ugly phrases such as *ballpark figures*, *one hundred and ten per cent* and *end of the day*. It simply would not cross their minds to mangle English in this way. Think about what you want to say before you write; think about how you would like it to sound to the reader. Write and say what you mean. And enjoy the words of the English language – they are a fine heritage.

Pretentious, Moi?

We have adopted a great many foreign phrases into English because, despite the vast size of our vocabulary, a foreign word or phrase sometimes captures something that would take a great deal of explaining in English. Take double entendre *(which is not even the French term),* chutzpah *or* angst. *All of these make immediate sense to the reader, whereas an English explanation would be wordy and cumbersome. As always, it is a matter of common sense whether or not to use a foreign phrase or to stay with an English expression. Orwell was famous for his taut, lucid style and he may have felt that the use of foreign phrases smacked of pretention and downgraded our own language to some extent.*

Appendix 1: Frequently Misspelled Words

abscess (*-bsc-*)

accommodate (2 *c*s and 2 *m*s)

acquaint (not 'aquaint')

aerial (not 'arial' or 'ariel')

aquiline (not 'acquiline')

arctic (not 'artic' – unless short for 'articulated lorry')

benighted (not 'beknighted')

Britannia (1 *t*, 2 *n*s)

Britannica (1 *t*, 2 *n*s)

Brittany (2 *t*s, 1 *n*)

broccoli (not 'brocolli')

conscientious (the root word is 'science')

consensus (not 'concensus')

desiccated (not 'dessicated')

desperate (not 'desparate')

drunkenness (double *n*)

exercise (not 'excercise')

ecstasy (not 'extasy' nor 'extacy')

espresso (not 'expresso')

February (not 'Febuary')

glamorize, glamorous (not 'glamourize/-ous')

graffiti (not 'grafitti')

gauge (not 'guage')

harass (not 'harrass')

idiosyncrasy (not 'idiosyncracy')

itinerary (not 'itinery')

kerb (meaning pavement edge, not 'curb' in UK)

led (past tense of 'to lead')

liaise, liaison (not 'liase', 'liasion')

lightening (making less heavy)

lightning (flash – not 'lightening')

liquefy (not 'liquify')

Mediterranean (not 'Meditteranean')

memento (not 'momento')

millennium (not 'millenium')

minuscule (not 'miniscule')

mischievous (not 'mischievious')

pejorative (not 'perjorative')

pharaoh (not 'pharoah')

Portuguese (not 'Portugese')

restaurateur (not 'restauranteur')

sacrilege (not 'sacrilege')

separate (not 'seperate')

stiletto (not 'stilleto')

supersede (not 'supercede')

threshold (not 'threshhold')

withhold (not 'withold')

you're ('you are')

your (meaning 'belonging to you')

Appendix 2: Commonly Confused Words

As the English language has somewhere in the region of one million words, it is almost inevitable that we are going to confuse similarly written or similar-sounding words and phrases from time to time. Here is a list of some commonly confused words.

Accept/Except Consent to/Excluded

Adverse/Averse Contrary to, hostile/Opposed to

Affect/Effect (1) Verb: produce an effect on, influence/to bring about (2) Noun: psychological term for emotion that effects behaviour/result or consequence

Alternate/Alternative Two things succeeding each other in turn/Another option

Allusions/Illusions Referring to/Imaginary, false ideas

All together/Altogether All in one place/Totally

Amoral/Immoral/Immortal Without moral principles/Morally wrong/Living for ever

Aural/Oral Relating to the ear/Relating to the mouth

Avenge/Revenge Inflict retribution for another/Retaliation in the name of justice

Born/Borne Come into existence/Carried

Brooch/Broach Piece of jewellery/Raise a subject for discussion

Canvas/Canvass Coarse fabric/Solicit votes

Censer/Censure/Censor Container in which incense is burned/Criticize sharply/Suppress unsuitable or inflammatory material

Childish/Childlike Immature/Having the qualities of a child

Compel/Impel Bring about by force/Drive forward by force

Complimentary/Complementary Giving praise *or* free of charge/Something that completes or goes together with

Currant/Current Dried fruit/Belonging to the present time; flow of water, electricity

Deduce/Deduct Draw a logical conclusion/Take away

Disinterested/Uninterested Without bias/Indifferent

Dominate/Domineer Exercise control over/Act in an arrogant way

Elder/Older The older one of a group/having lived longer

Egotism/Egoism Self-obsession/Philosophy of self-interest

Emigrate/Immigrate Leave one's home to settle elsewhere/Go into a country intending to be a resident

Empathy/Sympathy Identifying with and understanding the plight of another/Having a shared feeling with another

Exercise/Exorcize Physical activity or application of the mind for its development/Expel an evil spirit

Flammable/Inflammable These both mean the same: easily set fire to

Flout/Flaunt Show contempt (for authority)/Show off

Forgo/Forego Go without/Go first in place or time

Founder/Flounder Sink (of a ship)/Struggle in a task

Gourmet/Gourmand Connoisseur of good food/A glutton

Grisly/grizzly/gristly Horrifying or disgusting/Grey-haired/Containing gristle (usually applied to meat)

Historic/Historical Important or famous in history/Connected to the past

Hoard/Horde A store that has been hidden away/A large group or gang

Illegible/Unreadable Not readable due to its appearance/Not readable due to its dullness or difficulty

Illicit/Elicit Secret and unlawful/Draw out (a response)

Imply/Infer Hint or insinuate/Reach a conclusion

Insidious/Invidious Progressing in a harmful, secretive way/Likely to cause resentment against the perpetrator of a [seeming] injustice

It's/Its It is/Belonging to it

Lie/Lay To repose horizontally or tell a fib/To place (something or a person somewhere)

Lose/Loose Misplace/Not tight

Luxurious/Luxuriant Sumptuous/Lush and profuse in growth (vegetation, etc.)

Misanthrope/Misogynist One who hates humankind/Hater of women

Passed/Past Moved onward/Belonging to a former time

Pedal/Peddle Foot-operated lever, to use pedal/To sell goods (often illegally), to sell a view or idea (used derogatorily)

Plane/Plain Flat surface, airplane/Undecorated, ordinary, a flat area of land

Portentous/Pretentious Acting like an omen/Claiming more merit or importance than is due

Prophecy/Prophesy A prediction of future events/The verb of same; to foretell events

Principal/Principle Head of an organization, chief/Code of conduct, guiding truth

Proceed/Precede Make one's way, continue/To go before in order of time, importance, etc.

Prostrate/Prostate Lying horizontally (usually overcome by grief or exhaustion)/Gland in male reproductive system

Rapt/Wrapped To have one's attention fully absorbed/enveloped

Sensual/Sensuous Depending on or delighting the physical senses/Relating to the senses

Stationery/Stationary Paper and envelopes/Remain still

Swat/Swot Hit hard and abruptly/Study hard

Their/They're/There Belonging to them/They are/In that place

Too/To Also, as well/Part of infinitive verb (*to be*, *to do*, or example), also preposition of direction (*go to*)

Tortuous/Torturous Full of twists and turns/Inflicting agony

Troop/Troupe A company assembled; soldiers/Company of acrobats or actors

Urban/Urbane Pertaining to a city/Sophisticated

Urban fox

Urbane fox

Use/Usage To bring into service/Habitual practice (grammatical)

Waiver/Waver Refrain from insisting on something/Be irresolute or unsteady

Whose/Who's Belonging to whom/Who is

Yolk/Yoke Yellow part of an egg/Shoulderpiece for carrying, with connotations of servitude or slavery

Further Reading

Amis, Kingsley, *The King's English*, HarperCollins, 1997

Bierce, Ambrose, *The Devil's Dictionary*, Dover Publications Inc., 1993

Bryson, Bill, *Mother Tongue*, Penguin Books, first paperback edition, 1991

Bryson, Bill, *Troublesome Words*, Penguin Books, first paperback edition, 1997

Butterfield, Jeremy, *Damp Squid*, OUP hardback edition, 2008; paperback edition, 2009

Chambers Essential English Grammar and Usage, Chambers, 1999

Cook Vivian, *Accomodating Brocolli in the Cemetary: Or Why Can't Anybody Spell?*, Profile Books, 2004

Crystal, David, *Rediscover Grammar*, Longman, first edition, 1988; Longman second edition, 2004

Crystal, David, *The Cambridge Encyclopedia of the English Language*, Cambridge University Press, illustrated edition, 1995; third edition, 2010

Crystal, David, *Who Cares About English Usage?* Penguin Books, 1984; second revised edition, 2000

Crystal, David, *Words, Words, Words*, OUP, 2007

Essinger, James, *Spellbound,* Robson Books, illustrated edition, 2006; Delta, 2007

Fowler, H. W., *A Dictionary of Modern English Usage,* OUP (Oxford) third edition, Birchfield, 1996

Hart, Horace H., *Hart's Rules for Compositors and Readers at the University Press*, OUP 1893; thirty-ninth edition, 1983

Heffer, Simon, *Strictly English*, Random House Books, 2010

Hitchings, Henry, *The Secret Life of Words*, John Murray, 2008

Humphrys, John, *Lost for Words*, Hodder Paperbacks, 2005

Jarvie, Gordon, *Bloomsbury Grammar Guide: Grammar Made Easy*, Bloomsbury Publishing PLC, revised edition, 2000

Lamb, Bernard C., *The Queen's English*, Michael O'Mara Books Ltd, 2010

Liberman, Anatoly, *Word Origins*, OUP (USA), 2005

Martin, Andrew (editor), *Funny You Should Say That,* Penguin Books, 2005

Parkinson, Judy, *I Before E (Except after C)*, Michael O'Mara Books, reprint edition, 2007

Pearsall, Judy and Trumble, Bill (editors), *The Oxford Reference Dictionary,* OUP, second edition, 2002

Taggart, Caroline and Wines, J. A., *My Grammar and I (Or Should That Be 'Me'?): Old-School Ways to Sharpen Your English*, Michael O'Mara Books, 2008

Taylor, Andrew, *A Plum in Your Mouth*, HarperCollins, 2006

Further Reading

Trenga, Bonnie, *The Curious Case of the Misplaced Modifier,* Writer's Digest Books, 2006

Truss, Lynne, *Eats, Shoots and Leaves*, Profile Books first edition, 2003

Walsh, Bill, *Lapsing into a Comma*, McGraw-Hill Contemporary, 2000

Wines, J. A., *Mondegreens: A Book of Mishearings,* Michael O'Mara Books, 2007

Index